Trade and FDI Related Reforms in the States, 1991-2007

Published in association with
Observer Research Foundation
New Delhi

Observer Research Foundation (ORF) is a public policy think-tank that aims to influence formulation of policies for building a strong and prosperous India. The ORF pursues these goals by providing informed and productive inputs, in-depth research and stimulating discussion. The Foundation is supported in its mission by a cross-section of India's leading public figures, academics and business leaders.

ABOUT THE AUTHOR

Gitanjali Sen is a Ph.D in Economics from University of Missouri-Columbia, USA. After teaching at a management institute in Bangalore (2004-05), she moved to Comat Technologies as Lead Economist. In the latter, she worked with Poverty Action Lab in socioeconomic impact evaluation of technological interventions in the Public Distribution System. She joined ORF in 2008 as a fellow, working in areas of state level policies to begin with. Her current project is on affirmative action in higher education, funded by ESRC.

Her areas of interests include: education, affirmative action, returns to education, child labour, status of marginal communities, corruption and socioeconomic impact evaluation of public programmes.

Trade and FDI Related Reforms in the States, 1991-2007

The Case of Maharashtra

GITANJALI SEN

ACADEMIC FOUNDATION
NEW DELHI

First published in 2010
by

ACADEMIC FOUNDATION
4772-73 / 23 Bharat Ram Road, (23 Ansari Road),
Darya Ganj, New Delhi - 110 002 (India).
Phones : 23245001 / 02 / 03 / 04.
Fax : +91-11-23245005.
E-mail : books@academicfoundation.com
www. academicfoundation.com

in association with the

Observer Research Foundation, New Delhi

Cataloging in Publication Data--DK
Courtesy: D.K. Agencies (P) Ltd. <docinfo@dkagencies.com>
Sen, Gitanjali.
Trade and FDI related reforms in the states, 1991-2007 : the case of Maharashtra / Gitanjali Sen.
p. cm.
Includes bibliographical references (p.).
ISBN 13: 9788171888252
ISBN 10: 8171888259

1. Maharashtra (India)--Commercial policy. 2. Investments, Foreign--India--Maharashtra. 3. India--Economic policy–1991- I. Title. II. Title: Trade and foreign direct investment related reforms in the states, 1991-2007.

DDC 381.095479 22

Typeset by Italics India, New Delhi.

Printed and bound in India.

Contents

List of Tables, Figures and Appendices

Tables

Figures

Appendices

Foreword

It has been well documented that trade reforms in India did not follow a well thought-out path of national strategy, and that, from the eighties reforms have been reactions to global triggers. Under the overall umbrella of liberalisation after 1991, trade as a percentage of GDP grew, and now accounts for close to 38 per cent of GDP, a tripling in the last two decades. During this period, India primarily adopted a policy of *sui generic* reforms in tariffs, laws and procedures, and the gradual dismantling of tariff barriers up to 2004 had much to do with the rapid growth of inward and outward trade. India acceded to the Marrakech agreements more or less unwillingly, but subsequently used the international commitment obligations to push through a number of reforms including those mandated by the TRIPs agreement. In short, the path has been determined more by national policy and priorities and less by any well-thought strategy of trade competitiveness.

There is a notable exception to this, and that is in the services sector. In the field of technology and software, India realised its competitive advantages as a large number of Indian companies expanded their footprints in the developed countries. Tariff and tax concessions as well as a focus on computer education helped India to achieve a pre-eminence in the field of software delivery, a position that has yet to be challenged.

The interesting developments during this period were that the action for liberalisation of trade was focused entirely in Delhi in the Central government. Even during the trade negotiations that led to the WTO agreements, there were little consultations with the States. There was also the complaint that even Parliament had been kept in the dark about several of the WTO commitments. The roadblock to progress under the Doha round, that are primarily focused on agriculture, owe their origins to the lack of these state-level consultations in the early nineties.

In these circumstances, different states adopted different coping strategies to deal with the wave of liberalisation that was sweeping down from Delhi. Some states like West Bengal, resisted, others, most notably Maharashtra, Tamil Nadu and Gujarat, among others, welcomed the new policies and adapted to encourage industry and trade blossom in their geography. There has been little attempt to study state-level policies, and the extent to which individual states took advantage of a liberal tariff regime to encourage industrial development.

Gitanjali's study is an important attempt to fill this gap. In examining the role of industries in Maharashtra and the policies of the Government, she has attempted to trace the history of Maharashtra's development in the last two decades against the backdrop of national trade policies. It is an excellent attempt, and is an important contribution to the literature on the subject. It illustrates, very simply, how states can leverage Central government initiatives to the advantage of their citizens.

Her scholarship and diligence is to be commended, and it is hoped that there would be similar studies of other states that are generated from this exercise.

—Dr. S. Narayan

IAS (Retd.), President, Center for Asia Studies

Acknowledgments

My sincere thanks to Razeen Sally for sharing his knowledge at every step of this study. I am grateful to S. Narayan for his help with few important contacts relevant to the work. Also, my appreciation for all those who spared their precious time during the meetings related to this work. I owe thanks to Aseema Sinha for her thoughtful comments on an earlier version of this work. Finally, I acknowledge the financial and other administrative assistance of Observer Research Foundation during the period of study. I remain responsible for any errors.

Overview

The liberalisation policy of India that was initiated in 1991 was designed to dismantle the protectionist regime through removal of industrial licences, thereby reducing the strict bureaucratic control under which the country's foreign trade had been suffering for decades. The Import and Export (Control) Act of 1947 was replaced by the Foreign Trade (Development and Regulation) Act of 1992, empowering the Central government to announce and amend the export and import policy, or trade policy as it is called. The export-import policy was further liberalised several more times with the introduction of substantial concessions to boost agricultural exports, as well as initiatives of export promotion and the setting up of industrial parks. The unilateral initiative of liberalisation was later supported by commitments made under the World Trade Organisation (WTO) regime, and further liberalisation of imports through removal of import licences, quotas and quantitative restrictions.

The federal division of power between the Central and state governments in India allows the Central government to formulate trade policy. The state governments remain primarily as the implementing bodies. With the same liberalised trade policy announced for all states and union territories of the country, the impact of policy on export-import, inflow of foreign direct investment and growth rates vary largely among states, partly due to the difference in state initiatives supporting them.

The response to liberalisation policies followed by the WTO mandate at the Union level, and its impact on the overall economy, has been broadly discussed in several studies. This particular study attempts to analyse how the state of Maharashtra has fared in changing its trade-related policies and the implementation, in response to economic reforms that were implemented during the period of 1991-2007. Here, I define 'trade-related policies' as those policies and initiatives of the state government that affect international trade of the country or support the trade policy of the Centre.

This includes state-level tax policies, initiatives to attract foreign or domestic investors in the state, export promotion initiatives and development initiatives affecting business and investment in the state. It also discusses the changing role of business in the state, the bureaucratic mechanism working towards implementation of policies, the role of political parties of the state, and the role of chief minister as a leader of the state in framing and implementing trade-related policies.

The business climates across states of India vary to some extent due to the difference in state-level bureaucracy. Getting government approval for business or to set up plants, getting environment clearance, getting utility connections, and all other related procedures, take time of different lengths across different states in India. Some states are a little ahead of their counterparts in these respects, because of their various initiatives including e-governance, or the creation of a single-window system for all required clearances. These initiatives work to attract investments in the state and to increase the contribution of the state in the volume of international trade. Maharashtra, the subject of this case study, has been among the forerunners in some of these initiatives, along with the states of Gujarat, Andhra Pradesh and Tamil Nadu. Maharashtra is currently in the process of creating a single window clearance system for industries.

Maharashtra has been able to attract investors primarily through various incentive schemes and the development of several industrial clusters. According to industrial bodies, however, most investors would rather see more of the long-term development of infrastructure required for the industries than the setting up of incentives.

As things are, Maharashtra has in place a certain amount of reliable infrastructure. It has one of the best road and railway networks across India and houses two of the country's major ports. There remain concerns, however, including the increasing amount of port traffic and the delay in issuance of clearances at ports. Since international trade and investment has direct links to the availability of port facility, the state government should work to reduce the amount of turnaround time at port, along with more efficient issuance of clearances. Moreover, the state government must take proactive measures in making labour laws more flexible in order to encourage the flow of foreign investments into the state, keeping in mind that the Centre is unable to repeal laws without state approval.

In most of the electoral terms thus far, the leading party of the state of Maharashtra—either the coalition or the single party—had some representation in the Central government. This helps to maintain good relationship with the Centre. However, when we look at the state leadership, none of the political leaderships in Maharashtra has been as exemplary as those of the states of Gujarat or Andhra Pradesh, where the chief ministers were showcased as leaders in their respective states' reform initiatives. The case of one of the largest automobile corporations in the country, based in Maharashtra, indicates that if the state leadership has a larger say in the cabinet then that facilitates implementation of any project.

The example of Enron project provides a lesson calling for political stability in state leadership. Enron Corporation from the USA signed a MoU to build a power plant in Dabhol in 1992. From the very beginning, this project raised controversies from the point of non-competitive bidding, inefficiency and high tariff rate. Finally, the project had to be scrapped in 2001 after 95 per cent of its completion. This case also highlights the fact that when a state is ruled by a coalition government then sometimes, major decisions are taken while keeping the political interest of all partner parties in mind.

In this study, the performance of the state of Maharashtra has also been analysed by looking at some major macroeconomic indicators affecting business. An examination was also made of whether state policy was effective enough to take advantage of liberalisation or it was, by nature, more protective.

The following were considered as major indicators for this present study: growth indicators of the state; patterns of revenue receipts in the state; patterns of state financing; governance and institutional regulatory/ quality indicators; and the availability of physical infrastructure. The growth indicators indicate that Maharashtra stands among India's leading states, with the highest figures for state domestic product and its rate of growth. The ratio of debt to gross state domestic product (GSDP) has increased over the years, indicating higher amount of borrowing, primarily for public projects. The state is ranked sixth in the Index for Social and Economic Infrastructure, lagging behind states like Tamil Nadu, Gujarat and Kerala. Finally, the study includes two sectoral case studies: one on automobiles and auto component industry, and another on the pharmaceutical industry.

The objective of the present study is to explain how all these factors have worked in Maharashtra in the growth and development of those sectors. The study reveals that Maharashtra has been a major hub for automobile and auto components companies for the last few decades, due to several factors, including: the closeness of ports and good connectivity; availability of skilled manpower and designing, training institutes; state-level initiatives to attract investors and most important of all, the forward and backward linkages for the industry. However, the state needs to be more proactive in the coming years through development of infrastructure, if Maharashtra intends to stand in competition with states like Uttarakhand and Tamil Nadu for attracting FDI. The development of Maharashtra's pharmaceutical industry can also be attributed to the availability of skilled manpower and state-level initiatives through development of specialised industrial areas. The state has also announced a separate Biotechnology Policy, which brings some benefits to the investors in pharmaceutical sector as well. But the sustained development of this industry perhaps needs strong initiatives by the state in order to boost research and development, particularly in areas contributing to intellectual properties, rather than concentrating only on services like contract research and manufacturing or clinical research.

A brief policy prescription, along with a list of recommendations, concludes this study. These recommendations are being made in order to assist policymakers, investors and business houses alike in learning from the past and making those lessons work for an improved economy.

1 Introduction

India's policy towards economic reform, along with trade liberalisation, was announced by the government in 1991 amidst the fiscal and balance of payment crisis facing the country at that time. Over the last two decades, economists, policymakers, political leaders and business houses, have all had a major interest on how India has behaved amidst these initiatives and their overall impact on trade and related activities.

Indian federation is divided into three areas for purposes of jurisdiction, namely: one exclusively for the Union; one for the state government and the other, as dual responsibility of state and Centre. Trade policy is drafted at the union level and is formulated in export and import policies. There are certain aspects of it that are the prerogative of state government. Therefore, if the impact of liberalisation is to be studied in detail with respect to trade policy, the role of state governments in the making of trade policy and its implementation becomes an important area of examination.

This particular study opens with a brief explanation of the Central government's economic reform initiatives as reflected in its trade policy during the period of 1991-2007. It is in such context that an analysis is then made about how the state of Maharashtra has fared in changing its trade-related policies, and their implementation, in the same period. In the process, the study also explores how the state of Maharashtra has performed with respect to various general economic indicators that give us a picture of the state's overall initiative towards reform. Here, the term 'trade-related policies' is defined as those policies and initiatives of the state government that affect international trade, or are a consequence of the Centre's trade policy. While all economic sectors are regarded as important, this study puts more focus on the industrial and service sectors, and less on agriculture.

Previous studies have sought out to discuss the response to liberalisation policies followed by the World Trade Organization (WTO) mandate at the union level, and its overall impact on the economy. These authors include Joshi and Little (1996), Mukherji (2005), Mathur (2006), and Panagariya (2008), to name a few. In his study of the state's role in meeting WTO commitments, Jenkins (2003) argues that WTO, being an external actor actually reduces the autonomy of state governments. He suggests that even though state governments have little influence in WTO's other main functions—such as trade policy monitor and dispute settlement—they could have active WTO cells helping the Centre in such matters. The political economy scenario during democratic reform process explored by Jenkins (1999) is also relevant for discussion in the reform initiatives of state government. He makes the point that carrying on a sustainable reform policy in a democratic setting is theoretically difficult because of the presence of what he called powerful 'opponents of reform'. Jenkins finds that the fears of various sectors—farmers about losing subsidies, protected industrialists about facing foreign competition, and party leaders fearing the possibility of losing office—have all manged to create some kind of linkages with the electoral constituency, which could probably be mobilised against any policy reform.

Kumar and Kumar (1996), for their part, refer to cases of bureaucratic hurdles in economic reform. Meanwhile, Chari and Gupta (2007) in their study of the role of state-owned firms in policy-making, find that there are influences of state-owned firms in protecting their own industry from foreign investments; the state-owned firms are found to be more successful than private firms in influencing policymakers in preventing foreign entry. That study, however, is not focused on trade-related policies and makes little discussion on policy implementation issues at the state level that have a direct impact on international trade.

Several studies have established a link between Indian federalism and economic reform. For example, Rudolph and Rudolph (2001) broadly discuss the policy initiatives of the state of Andhra Pradesh towards reform, and Mathur (2005) analyses the impact of globalisation policies in cities, although not specifically about trade-related policies. Saez (2002) and Sinha (2004a), meanwhile, argue that there has been change in Centre-state economic relations after reform in terms of the type of competition among states. Saez (2002) explains that the change in Centre-state relation was 'from inter-governmental cooperation to inter-jurisdictional competition'. Sinha (2004a) explains the change to be from 'vertical competition to a horizontal competition', in which states compete with each other for resources from a wide variety of sources, rather than to acquire from centrally funded ones. Other studies have looked into economic reforms at state level, mostly to bring out comparisons among states in their reform initiatives, including, Babu (2002), Jenkins (2003), Kennedy (2004), Sinha (2004b), and Venkatesan and Verma (2000). Banerjee and Arunachalam (2007: 202-20) have put together post-reform studies of a few Indian states, including one study on Maharashtra, where the latter involves discussion on state of industrialisation, industrial sickness, state revenues, budgetary position, few social programmes and FDI, to some extent. But none of these earlier literature had focused on policy initiatives at the state level that affects trade policy, or that are outcomes of such trade policy. NCAER (2003) studies the differences in inter-state tax collection policy in India.

The present study distinguishes itself from existing literature on two counts. Firstly, after a brief discussion of the changes in union trade policy, this study limits its focus to those state-level policies which are either a direct consequence of international trade policy or affect the union trade policy. Hence, the primary focus is on how a particular state of India has fared in changing and implementing its own policy related to international trade during the liberalisation process. Moreover, this study covers only the state of Maharashtra whereas, I have not come across any study focusing on Maharashtra on the aspects mentioned above. The next few sections of the study are organised thus:

- Chapter II discusses the major features of union trade policy during the period of interest.
- Chapter III analyses the state-level policy changes in this period, along with the institutional influences on the policy change and its implementation. This section deals with the political economy aspect of public policy. In this chapter, areas under state list, union list and concurrent list, are identified in order to understand the federal distribution of power regarding the trade policy and its implementation. Here, discussion is restricted to trade and FDI-related issues, keeping in mind the need to understand how much

power has been exercised by states in trade-related policies during the reform initiative. A brief explanation is made about the state decision-making process on relevant trade-related policies to understand how a state interacts with the Centre; the agencies in the state responsible for implementing policies; and their capacity of implementation.

Moreover, this chapter describes the role of different interest groups, such as party or coalition politics, the role of a chief minister as state leader, influence of business on state policy-making, and capacity of the state bureaucracy in state-level decision-making and implementation regarding trade-related policies. While the role of leading political parties in state and coalition politics is being discussed, there is also an attempt to link the changes in power at the Centre and state, the relations between the ruling parties in both, and the nature of reform initiatives under different political scenarios.

- Chapter IV studies the impact of the trade-related policies in Maharashtra and the overall performance of the state during the period of economic liberalisation. Here, reference is made to studies conducted by the World Bank Doing Business Indicators, Investment Climate Assessment Survey of World Bank, Doing Trade Indicator, and primarily some indicators developed by Debroy and Bhandari (2005). From the indicators used in these studies, those that are relevant to state-level policies are selected, as they can help in the understanding of the domestic business or political climate of states. The few areas such as regulation, infrastructure, tax and custom administration, taxes, macroeconomic instability, access to land, and skill shortage, are explored to examine if those serve as major obstacles to investment in the state of Maharashtra.
- Chapter V contains a sectoral case study on the automobile and auto component industry of Maharashtra.
- Chapter VI is devoted to the case of the state's pharmaceutical industry.
- Chapter VII concludes the study with policy prescription and recommendations, followed by a list of references and the appendices.

2 Union Trade Policy

Introduction

This chapter discusses the changes in union trade policy during the period between 1991 and 2007, as that helps in the understanding of trade liberalisation initiatives of the Union government. Later, when a discussion is made about the liberalisation initiative of the state government of Maharashtra, those will be related better if there is knowledge of major trade policy changes at the Centre. This chapter is organised as follows:

- Section II summarises the external and internal reform initiatives of the Centre through few major changes in trade policy.
- Section III deals with the liberalisation initiative on certain goods, implemented unilaterally post 1991.
- Section IV deals with the unilateral liberalisation of services, along with FDI liberalisation during the same period.
- Section V focuses on GATT, WTO and Uruguay rounds.
- Section VI is a discussion of major bilateral and regional trade agreements.
- Section VII outlines some major export promotion initiatives of the Centre, along with the SEZ policy, implementing some of which is in states' purview.
- Section VIII concludes the chapter.

Economic Liberalisation: Internal and External Trade in Brief

Foreign trade in India suffered from bureaucratic hurdles and discretionary control till the middle of 1991, when the government came to the realisation that trade policies had to be liberalised in order to promote and develop foreign trade. The Foreign Trade (Development and Regulation) Act of 1992 replaced the Import and Export (Control) Act of 1947, in effect empowering the Central government to formulate the export and import policy in a timely manner.

Until the economic reforms were initiated in 1991, the bulk of international trade in India was protected by some types of quantitative restrictions, at the least.[1] About 94 per cent of agricultural goods, and 90 per cent of manufactured intermediate and capital goods, used to be covered by the quantitative restrictions. Therefore, at the beginning of the 1990s, there were several categories of importers, import licences and methods of importing that made India's trade policy complex. But with the substitution of Import-Export Policy of 1990-1993 by the Export and Import Policy (1992-1997) effectively from April 1992, the trade policy became easily comprehensible as the contents were brought down to one-tenth of the earlier size. It included the negative list of imports subject to licensing, instead of a long list of items allowed to import. However, almost all the consumer goods continued to require import licensing. The major external policies supporting liberalisation were simplification of tariff, elimination of quantitative restrictions on imports, reduction of export restriction and simplification of import licensing. Among the major internal reforms, the few to be mentioned were reduced control over locational and industrial licensing along with loosening of controls administered on prices in some sectors. In a 2002 WTO trade policy review, the Government of India estimated that an annual export growth of 12 per cent was required to raise the country's share of world trade to 1 per cent from the then existing rate of 0.67 per cent. Policies were thus directed to expanding export growth, too. The move towards a more open economy during post-liberalisation can be better understood from a few indices given in Table 2.1.

It must be noted that in the 15 years of reference period of liberalisation, import duties have come down drastically, along with a rise in trade and foreign investment figures. The liberalisation policy seems to have contributed to a rise in foreign currency reserves as well.

1. See Joshi and Little (1996).

Table 2.1

Towards a More Open Economy

	1990-91	*2005-06*
Peak import duties (manufactures)	200% plus	12.5%
Import controls	Tight, detailed	Negligible
Trade (goods)/GDP ratio (%)	14.6	32.7
Current receipts/GDP (%)	8.0	24.5
Software exports ($ billion)	Nil	23.6
Worker remittances ($ billion)	2.1	24.6
Foreign investment ($ billion)	Negligible	20.2
Foreign currency reserves ($ billion, as on March 31st)	2.2	145.1
Debt service ratio (%)	35.3	10.2

Source: WTO Trade Policy Review, reported by India in April 2007.

Unilateral Trade Liberalisation Trends Post-1991

As a move towards unilateral trade liberalisation, the 1992-93 budget announced elimination of import licensing in most capital goods, raw materials, intermediates and components, through a liberalised Exchange Rate Management System. It introduced a dual exchange rate system in which exporters got the weighted average of official rate and market rate. To make up for any losses arising as exporters' tax, the exchange rate adjustment and reduction in tariff was introduced in this budget. The exchange rate reform of 1993 unified exchange rates and transactions on the trade account were freed from foreign exchange control. In order to gradually expose Indian industries to global competition, the customs duties were also reduced in 1992-93. The Export-Import Policy announced in 1993 further focused on promoting exports from agriculture and labour-intensive sectors in which India was enjoying comparative advantage.

According to Panagariya (2008), trade liberalisation efforts in India since the 1980s have been mostly dominated by its own recognition of benefits in moving towards an outward-oriented economy. India moved towards unilateral liberalisation through lower trade barriers without waiting for a 'reciprocal liberalisation' from either its trading partners, the International Monetary Fund (IMF) or World Bank. The tariff liberalisation restricted mainly to the industrial goods was primarily a unilateral effort, which has continued even under the current UPA government, when the overall liberalisation trajectory seems to have slowed down. The primary reason for the consistent tariff reduction over the period was that even when the government changed, the succeeding government in power never reversed these changes and rather continued to follow through them. However, the trade liberalisation effort was not as aggressive for a few industries, such as automobiles, which are still subject to a customs duty as high as 100 per cent, and few textile items, where duties exceed 10 per cent.

During the first decade after liberalisation, India continued to maintain a large number of incentive programmes for exports, which were targeted to compensate for import restrictions, creating a possibility of misallocation of resources. The income tax exemptions, subsidised credit, export insurance and guarantees, export promotion, marketing assistance schemes, and access to specific imports usually subject to restrictive licensing, were the major heads of this export-oriented initiative. For example, the profits earned through exports are not subject to tax; hence, it affects the nation's welfare in some way, which is probably worse than slapping tariffs. It eventually turns into a transfer from the exporting country to the importing country in terms of reduced prices that the latter shells out. However, in the Export-Import Policy of 2002-2007, the government has planned to encourage exports mainly through confining export restrictions to a few sensitive items, whereas export-import prohibitions are maintained only for health and security reasons.

Unilateral Services and FDI Liberalisation Post-1991

Substantial liberalisation was also initiated in the services sector through easing the foreign investment. In India, key sectors such as banking, insurance and telecommunications, have been controlled by government from the beginning. But the liberalisation initiative with 'negative list' approach has been an encouraging sign for domestic and foreign investment in service sectors. It allowed 100 per cent foreign investment in all sectors, subject to the sectoral rules and regulations, unless separate rules were mentioned in the FDI policy. In four sectors—namely, retail trading (except single-brand product retailing), atomic energy, lottery business, betting and other forms of gambling—FDI is completely prohibited. If a foreign investor has an equity share in excess of 24 per cent in manufacturing of an item reserved for small-scale sectors, or if he has an existing joint venture or technology transfer agreement or trademark agreement in the same field, then prior government approval is required. There are 28 listed sectors subject to sector-specific policies, and in those cases, sectoral caps on foreign investment may or may not go up to 100 per cent.

In order to promote competition and facilitate growth, Government of India has autonomously permitted 100 per cent FDI under automatic route in IT software and IT-enabled services. Considering telecommunications as an input into growing software and services sector, and thus critical for development, private investment was encouraged in the telecommunications sector. But this came without any institutional change in work ethic or procurement policy of government service providers to make them more efficient and provide them a level playing field before the entry of private investors. Any such reform in government service providers would have called for bureaucratic hurdles and pressure from trade unions. Even after allowing private investment in the telecommunication sector in 1992, it still took about 10 years for government to corporatise the department of telecommunication services when BSNL was allowed to work as an autonomous corporation to face private competition.[2]

The GATT/WTO: India's Commitments in Uruguay Round, Post-UR and FDI Liberalisation

The Uruguay Round (UR) of multilateral trade negotiations was launched in 1986 and concluded in Geneva on December 1993. The negotiations in these rounds of talks involved traditional General Agreement on Tariffs and Trade (GATT) subjects such as tariff and non-tariff measures, the improvement of GATT rules and disciplines on subsidies, safeguards, and further extended to cover additional areas such as trade related intellectual property rights (TRIPs), trade related investment measures (TRIMs), and trade in services. GATT attempted to reduce tariffs through several trade negotiations. But the flexibilities demanded by the developing countries in the draft of TRIPS and their dissatisfaction in the offer of developed countries in the issues related to agriculture, encouraged the developed countries to create a supposedly more institutionalised form, the WTO. India was a founding member of GATT (1947) and WTO, the latter being in force from January 1995.

2. See Mukherji (2005).

In the Uruguay Round, India opposed the negotiations for TRIPS as it did not realise the importance of protection of intellectual property in absence of trade orientation in the country and could not gauge its own competitiveness in fields like software and pharmaceuticals, at that time. Negotiations thus happened towards protecting the interest of developed countries, particularly the US pharmaceutical sector, with the grant of 20 years' worth of monopoly over product patent to innovators. For the same reason of initial opposition in negotiations on general agreement in trade in services, India could not deal as efficiently as the US in service negotiations, where it had a major potential of export earnings.

After the conclusion of Uruguay Round agreement, the US started to push for inclusion of labour and environmental standards in the WTO agenda, facing opposition from India and several other developing countries. Once again, four new issues—namely, investment, competition policy, government procurement and trade facilitation—were in the WTO study agenda in Singapore, and remained the most controversial point between developing and developed nations in the Doha Round of 2001. However, in 2003 at Cancun, the European Union agreed to concentrate only on the agenda of trade facilitation and left the Doha Round to focus primarily on trade liberalisation in agriculture, industry and services. The Doha Round concluded in 2006 with some positive outcomes. Trade facilitation through simplification, harmonisation and computerisation of customs clearance procedures, is one of the four Singapore issues on which negotiations are still ongoing.

In the Hong Kong ministerial conference of 2005, India, along with a few more developing nations, expressed interest in opening up their selected sectors. There are still certain areas, such as 'movement of natural persons' (Paragraph 4), that need to be sorted so that developing nations do not feel the threat of losing in the competition. The services sectors have witnessed accelerated growth in the last few decades, and India being ranked the 20th exporter in services, Paragraph 4 becomes an important issue for the country.

Bilateral and Regional Trade Agreements: A Summary

In the 1990s, the United States and European Union began aggressive negotiations under Preferential Trade Area (PTA) arrangement, to liberalise trade only with its partner countries and discriminate against non-members. India started its own unilateral liberalisation in the mid-1980s, when it lowered trade barriers indiscriminately. But after some time, amidst indications that the North American and European trading blocs were behaving in a discriminatory manner, India started negotiating on the regional trading arrangements or the PTAs.

The SAARC Preferential Trading Arrangement (SAPTA) between India, Pakistan, Bangladesh, Sri Lanka, Nepal, Bhutan and Maldives, came into force in 1995, seeking concessional duty on subcontinent trade. India signed a bilateral free trade agreement (FTA) with Sri Lanka in 2000, and three more FTAs with Singapore, Thailand and ASEAN in 2003. One major agreement towards creation of FTA in the Asian continent happened in the 12th SAARC Summit, leading to the formation of South Asian Free Trade Area (SAFTA). It came into being in 2006, agreeing for zero customs duty in the free-trade zone created between India, Pakistan, Bangladesh, Sri Lanka, Nepal and Maldives, by the year 2016.

India is party to several bilateral and regional free trade agreements. The fruits of those agreements, however, cannot be fully maximised due to several non-tariff barriers (NTBs) at both sides even in the absence of tariff. For example, Saquib and Taneja (2005) have identified non-tariff barriers faced by India's exports in Sri Lanka and ASEAN in the form of technical barriers to trade, or phytosanitary measures.

Among some other major bilateral agreements, the ones with Bhutan and Nepal have provided those countries preferential market access. A free trade agreement between India and Sri Lanka made operational in 2000 helped India in phasing out tariffs on most of the products except for a few in the negative list. A Comprehensive Economic Partnership Agreement (CEPA) between both countries initiated in 2004 covers negotiations in trade in services and investment. A preferential trading agreement was signed in 2003 for free movement of goods and services along with reduction in tariffs between India and Afghanistan. Another regional grouping named BIMST-EC between Bangladesh, India, Myanmar, Sri Lanka and Thailand was formed in 1997. The India-Singapore Comprehensive Economic Cooperation Agreement (CECA) was signed in 2005. India has also signed a framework agreement for CECA with

ASEAN, another between India and Thailand and a FTA on goods, services and investment being under negotiation.

Ideally, FTAs and tariff cut agreements should be preceded by investigations of domestic policies in the partner country. This will help mitigate the potential negative impacts of unfair competition, as imports would flood the local markets and thus threaten domestic businesses, as what happened in the case of auto components industry at the beginning of 2000 after a FTA with Thailand was signed in October 2003. The ongoing negotiations on FTA with the Gulf Cooperation Council (GCC), if concluded, may prove to be beneficial for both. Since 3 to 4 per cent of India's exports go to the six countries of this region, and 20 per cent of India's imports come from the same region, a FTA is expected to make a difference in international trade profile of both parties. In June 2007, India and EU began negotiations on bilateral trade in goods and services and in investment across all sectors of the economy. Another negotiation for CECA is currently ongoing between India and Malaysia, which is expected to be concluded in 2009. Some more preferential trading agreements or FTAs are under negotiations by India with Chile, Mauritius, Korea, Japan, China, MERCOSUR,[3] and SACU (Southern African Customs Union).

Even if India does not have as many FTAs as the European Union and US, still, the impact of so many bilateral agreements on India over the long run remains unclear. Certainly, the trade agreements come with some benefit to the member countries as opposed to their trading partner outside the agreement, but there are so many provisions under WTO that need to be extended to all its members equally that the net effectiveness of bilateral agreements becomes difficult to judge. For example, regarding removal of subsidies or following anti-dumping rules, a country may find it difficult to sort out the source of production accordingly before trading. Moreover, customs officials may find the calculation to be complicated in the case of special provision in removal of customs duty to a bilateral trading partner. Therefore, to minimise the risk of global welfare and in economies scale, the Doha Round of negotiations started discussion on factual presentation of all regional trading agreements, but in that process the developing

3. MERCOSUR is a Southern common market, which is a customs union between Brazil, Argentina, Uruguay, Paraguay and Venezuela, with Bolivia, Chile, Colombia, Ecuador and Peru having associated member status.

countries should not start from a different platform with respect to their developed counterparts.

Some Export Promotion Initiatives: SEZs

The EXIM policy of 1992-1997 gave importance to exports for agricultural and allied services in which the country holds comparative advantage. The following were the few major initiatives: permission of export oriented units (EOU) for agriculture and allied activities to avail of duty-free capital goods imports under the Export Oriented Unit/Export Processing Zones (EPZ) Scheme even if they export only 50 per cent of their output; reduction of negative list of exports; and introduction of Export Promotion of Capital Goods (EPCG) Scheme for the services sector for the first time. Also, the definition of 'capital goods' has been expanded to include sectors like agriculture, mining and services. The Electronic Hardware Technology Park (EHTP) Scheme was introduced, permitting 100 foreign investments in electronic sector and providing benefits at par with EOU/EPZ units. The modified EXIM policy of 1997-2002 announced two more initiatives, namely, Agriculture Export Processing Zones (AEZs) and Market Access Initiative (MAI). In the former, the state governments are supposed to identify the AEZs for export of specific products and develop a comprehensive package of services to be provided by the state government agencies, state agricultural universities, and all the institutions of Union government. In case of MAI, the Central government is supposed to assist the industry in research and development, market research, market and product-specific studies, warehousing and retail marketing infrastructure in select countries, direct market promotion activities through media advertising and buyer-seller meets.

The modified EXIM policy announced the creation of SEZs with a view to promote exports and attract larger foreign investment to India. The SEZ scheme is a special duty-free enclave, deemed as a foreign territory for trading activities and announced in 2000. Under this scheme, duty-free import or procurement from DTA (Domestic Tariff Area) of goods would be permitted for setting up of factory in these zones; the SEZ developers would be eligible for various entitlements under income tax act; SEZs would be permitted to subcontract part of their production through DTA or through other SEZ/EOU/EPZ/EHTP/STP (Software Technology Parks). Except for the SEZ scheme, there were only few modifications in EPCG scheme, duty exemption scheme, duty remission scheme, and EOU/EPZs/EHTPs/STPs announced in the same policy. There were no major export promotion initiatives freshly announced in the foreign trade policy of 2004-2009, replacing the EXIM policy of 2002-2007, except for the one in free trade and warehousing zone. The latter is supposed to create trade-related infrastructure to facilitate import and export of goods and services with freedom to conduct trade transactions in free currency. Upto 100 per cent FDI would be permitted to establish and develop infrastructure in these zones, where all the units would qualify for benefits available at SEZs. One important modification in export promotion scheme during this period was that imports of capital goods of any age have been allowed under EPCG scheme. Also, the EOUs have been exempted from service tax in proportion to their exported goods and services and they have been permitted to retain 100 per cent of export earnings in Export Earners Foreign Currency (EEFC) accounts under EOU/EHTP/STP/BTP schemes.

Although the SEZ Act became effective from 2005, its implementation has not been as expedient as expected. There are a few states, including Tamil Nadu, Maharashtra, Gujarat, Andhra Pradesh and West Bengal, who have taken initiatives in development of SEZs, with comparatively fewer initiatives in other states. The federal distribution of power in policy making and the implementation between Centre, state and local bodies, to be explained in the next chapter creates bureaucratic hurdles at times that needs to be addressed in order for these export promotion initiatives to succeed.

Concluding Note

The major programme of economic liberalisation initiated by the Government of India encouraged a larger flow of inward foreign investment and increased international trade. It helped India to achieve an annual average growth rate of about 6 per cent in 14 years of liberalisation till 2005. Initially, the growth rate was as good as 7 per cent between 1993 and 1996, which slowed down to 4.8 per cent during 1997-98. But due to the continued support towards liberalisation, it picked up to over 6 per cent for the next two consecutive years and went up to as high as 8.6 per cent on average between 2003 and 2006. According to the WTO trade policy review of 2007, India is the fourth largest economy after the US, China and Japan in terms of purchasing power parity (PPP) GDP, with a rise in its share in world GDP (PPP) from 4.3 per cent in 1991 to almost 6 per cent in 2005.

The trade policy changes post 1991 also strengthened external sector of the country, increasing the foreign exchange reserve above the US$ 100 billion level. This removed the fear against opening up the economy and proved to bring more efficiency and competitiveness with reduction of global transaction costs from fall of duty rates.

3 Policy Changes in Maharashtra

Institutional Influence and Implementation

Introduction

This chapter explores how the state of Maharashtra has fared in changing its trade-related policies and how it has done regarding implementation of the policies in response to the economic reform during the period of 1991-2007. It discuses how the state of Maharashtra has dealt with the central directives and rules regarding trade policy and the internal or regional compulsions, obstacles toward reform. The trade-related policies as defined earlier are the initiatives of state government that affect international trade, or are a consequence of trade policy of the Centre. This includes state-level tax policies, initiatives to attract foreign or domestic investors in the state, export promotion initiatives and developmental initiatives affecting business in the state. Hence, the chapter also discusses the role of different institutions in policy-making and the implementing bodies in Maharashtra involved in trade-related policies.

The next sections of this chapter are organised as follows:

- Section II discusses federal distribution of power between Centre and state related to international trade policy.
- Section III discusses the role of institutions, as well as non-institutional bodies of Maharashtra in decision-making and implementation of trade-related policies. It analyses the primary driving forces behind changes during this period of economic liberalisation through party-coalition politics, role of a chief minister as leader of the state, and capacity of the state bureaucracy.
- Section IV discusses state-level trade-related policies including industrial policy, SEZ policy and some related policies with status of implementation.
- Section V concludes the chapter with policy prescriptions.

Trade-Related Policies of States

Even as international trade policy is framed only at the Centre, there are certain indirect powers that states enjoy in framing and implementation of policy. The federal distribution of power demarcates certain areas in states' purview that are either a direct consequence of union trade policy or have an impact on international trade. This study defines those as trade related policy. As trade-related policies are discussed, it relates to both goods and services. Goods are split into manufacturing and agriculture, both having border and non-border barriers, whereas services are highly differentiated and the barriers are mainly the ones that are non-border regulatory. Union government is primarily responsible for policies in goods other than agriculture, and services as defined in the constitution; and agriculture falls under the state list along with its own set of areas in goods and services to be discussed in the next few paragraphs.

To map the federal distribution of power, Figure 3.1 lists policies linked to international trade directly or indirectly, that fall under the union category. These are framed at the Centre and states do not have any role in framing those policies, whereas responsibilities of implementing some of those lie with states. State can only frame its policies in line with union trade policy on the listed few in its own discretionary power, as stated in the state list in Figure 3.2. There are a few other areas as outlined in Figure 3.3 that are listed for both Centre and state, and named as concurrent areas.

Union List

Figure 3.1 identifies areas from trade policy that fall under the jurisdiction of the federal government covering the sectors of agriculture, manufacturing and services. In the above list, exim policy, customs-excise duties, SEZ policy are part of union trade policy, which have a direct effect on international trade. Union government also has the right to limit American Depository Receipts (ADR), Global Depository Receipts (GDR) and External Commercial Borrowings (ECB), to control the movement of foreign exchange in the country; this, in turn, has indirect effects on international trade. Exchange rate adjustments affect exports and imports. An appreciated domestic currency makes export costlier, imports cheaper and vice-versa for a depreciated domestic currency. Other direct and indirect taxes—such as income tax, wealth tax and corporate tax—affect production and business in the country, and thereby influence exports and imports indirectly. A business-friendly industrial policy attracts domestic and foreign investment, providing indirect support to international trade.

Figure 3.1

Union List

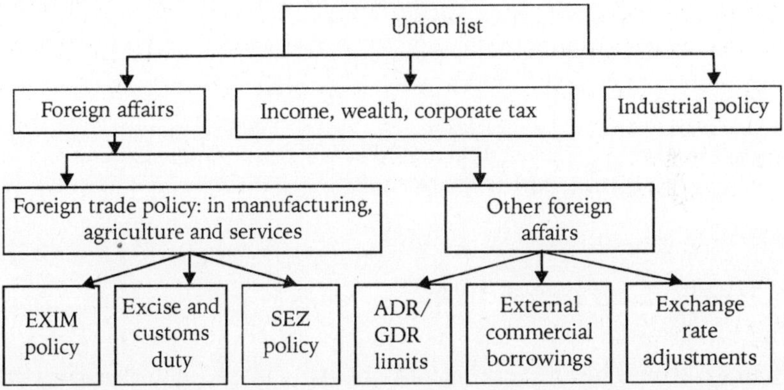

State List

Figure 3.2 provides a summary of the state list of trade-related areas. Agriculture being a state subject under the Constitution, some domestic reforms in operations can be done by the state. However, the policies on agricultural credit, agricultural prices and trade, are decided by the Centre. Any increase in state taxes—such as sales tax and service tax—acts as a deterrent to domestic production, business and vice-versa for any decrease in those. The excise tax, entry tax and octroi limit movements of goods to and from the state. All other fees such as stamp duty, registration fee, minimum licence fee for traders and market fees, act as sources of revenue for the state. More than the amount collected from those fees, however, the bureaucracy involved in the entire collection process becomes a discouraging factor for doing business in the state, and also in attracting investment. The responsibility of actual implementation of Industrial Entrepreneurs Memorandum (IEMs), SEZ policy, is in the hands of the Centre. It indirectly depends on state-level bureaucracy and political scenario as well, because the state has a role in recommending and providing several clearances, a point that will be discussed further in the latter part of this chapter.[1]

Figure 3.2

State List

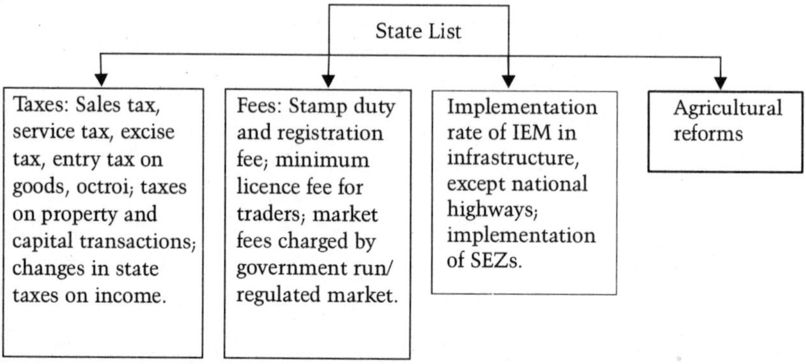

State taxes on income should not work as a discouraging factor in doing business in any state. As this tax may vary across states, its percentage should not be very high in any particular state, otherwise, there is a possibility of skilled people relocating to some other states where they will find less tax burden on their earnings.

Concurrent List

All three points mentioned in Figure 3.3 of concurrent list mainly affect domestic business scenario in any state and thus, in attracting investment into the state. For setting up any business in a state, the investor would look for flexible labour laws, good infrastructure and power supply, along with skilled labour. Once these issues are addressed, business comes easily into the state, increasing possibility of domestic and international trade.

Apart from the above categories under state list and concurrent list, implementation and effectiveness of trade policy is another area where state government plays a major role, as the exportable goods are produced in the states and sent outside only when those can beat the competition. To

1. Also, see Jenkins (1999, 2003), Kennedy (2004), Rudolph and Rudolph (2001), Saez (2000, 2002 and 2005), Sinha (2004a, 2004b), Venkatesan and Verma (2000) for sub-national analysis of India's liberalisation policies.

Figure 3.3

Concurrent List

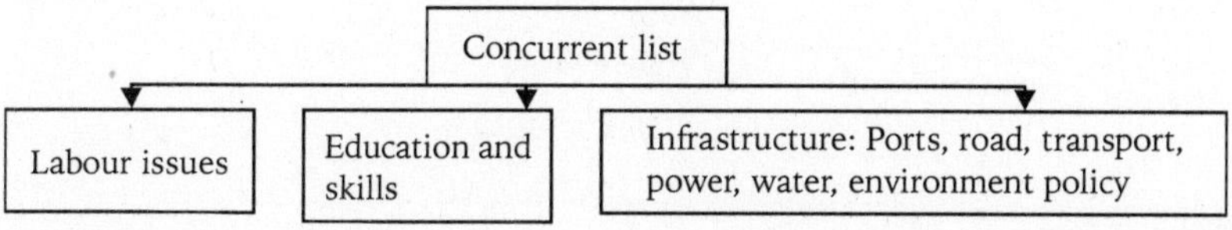

compete globally, the industrial units need to improve on product quality. They need to undertake technology and skill upgradation, diversification and design development, all of which help make export products competitive in the international market. Agricultural marketing, along with proper storage facility, food processing and commercial farming, are the areas where the state can help improving agricultural trade and reap the benefits of liberalisation. Special policy initiatives are required by the state to take advantage of its ports and wide seashores.

Therefore, for trade-related policies of interest, this study considers the ones from state list and concurrent list above—along with some powers lying with state—in implementation and effectiveness of foreign trade policy. The policies under union list remain beyond the scope of this study.

The next section will provide a clear picture on how Maharashtra gets involved in trade-related policies, with a detailed description of the institutions working on those policies and state implementing agencies.

Institutions Driving Trade-Related Policy Changes in Maharashtra

The bureaucratic system in practice and subsequent distribution of power in trade-related policies at state level as explained in Figure 3.4, helps in understanding which institutions are involved and how they work. A discussion will also be made about some non-institutional bodies that influence policy-making and implementation of trade-related policies in Maharashtra.

State Institutions

The state-level hierarchy for policy-making is associated with the political framework mandated in Article 40 of the Constitution of India. It was further strengthened by the law on Panchayat Raj through the 73rd Constitutional Amendment Act of 1992 and the 74th Constitutional Amendment Act of 1992.[2]

Figure 3.4

State-Level Hierarchy

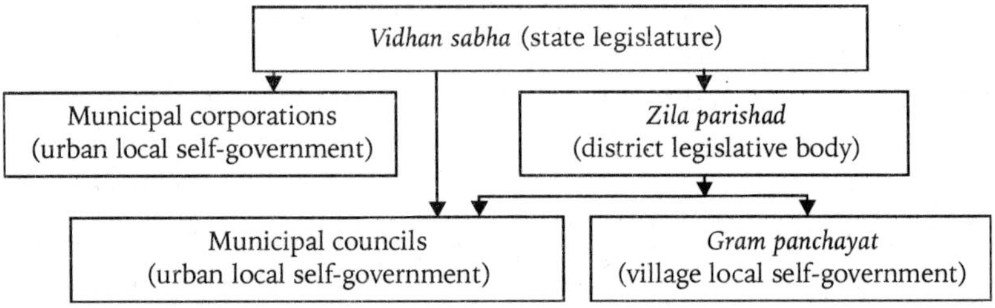

Source: "Local Governments in Asia and Pacific: A Comparative Study," UNESCAP, Human Settlements Country Paper: India, Figure 3.2.

As presented in Figure 3.4, the top-most elected representative in the state being *vidhan sabha*, both the local bodies that are, municipal corporations and municipal councils work under it. *Gram panchayat*, being another local body, works under *zila parishad*. Local bodies in states are supposed to improve the performance of the economy through proper utilisation of local resources and human potential. With economic liberalisation and rapid urban growth, the urban bodies are expected to have a bigger share of the responsibilities in improving the efficiency of programmes, services and in mobilising resources.

The Municipal Acts in India delineate the duties and responsibilities of municipal governments, which are either obligatory or discretionary in nature. Among those obligatory responsibilities, the few relevant to attracting foreign investors in the state are ensuring supply of pure and wholesome water; construction, maintenance, lightning and watering; cleansing of public streets, places and sewers; regulation of offensive, dangerous or obnoxious trades, callings or practices; maintenance or support of public hospitals and establishment of primary schools. Therefore, most of the administrative functions of state government for

2. UNESCAP (n.d.). "Local Governments in Asia and Pacific: A Comparative Study", *Human Settlements, Country Paper: India, http://www.unescap.org/huset/lgstudy/country/india/india.html*, accessed on 5 June 2009.

development of infrastructure are transferred to the local level. Hence, local-level bodies have an important role in implementation of trade-related policies because attracting investments in the state is directly related to the infrastructure conditions of the state and the prevailing level of bureaucracy (Babu, 2002).

The elected legislatures in states have control on state-level policy, own tax and revenue collection and self-determined expenditure allocations. The responsibilities towards collection of taxes that can be levied under the Constitution are divided among the Centre, state and the local bodies. The taxes collected by the Centre and state were the subject of an earlier part of this study; this time, it is the type of collection by local bodies that will be described. Urban local bodies, as permitted by the state acts, are responsible for collecting only the taxes on land and buildings, taxes on vehicles, entry tax on goods or octroi for use towards consumption and sale, theatre or show tax, and taxes on advertisements other than in newspapers.

Figure 3.5 maps the state-level institutions involved in areas of revenue collection, infrastructure in Maharashtra, and the respective acts for policy implementation.

In Maharashtra, the sales tax, service tax, excise tax, entry tax on goods and octroi, are administered at the state level by the Department of Sales Tax, Government of Maharashtra with the help of acts mentioned in Figure 3.5. The commissioner of sales tax appointed by state government has jurisdiction over the whole state in the matter of value added tax (VAT). No dealer is eligible to pay any tax under VAT 2005, unless he possesses a valid certificate of registration either under this act or under Bombay Sales Tax Act, 1959. Under VAT 2005, a refund is granted to the dealer purchasing or importing motor vehicles under the Maharashtra Tax on Entry of Motor Vehicles into the Local Areas Act, 1987 or under Maharashtra Tax on Entry of Goods into the Local Areas Act, 2002. Apart from these, municipal acts allow local authority to collect non-tax revenue through issuance of licences.

Figure 3.5

State-Level Institutions in Maharashtra in Trade-Related Policies

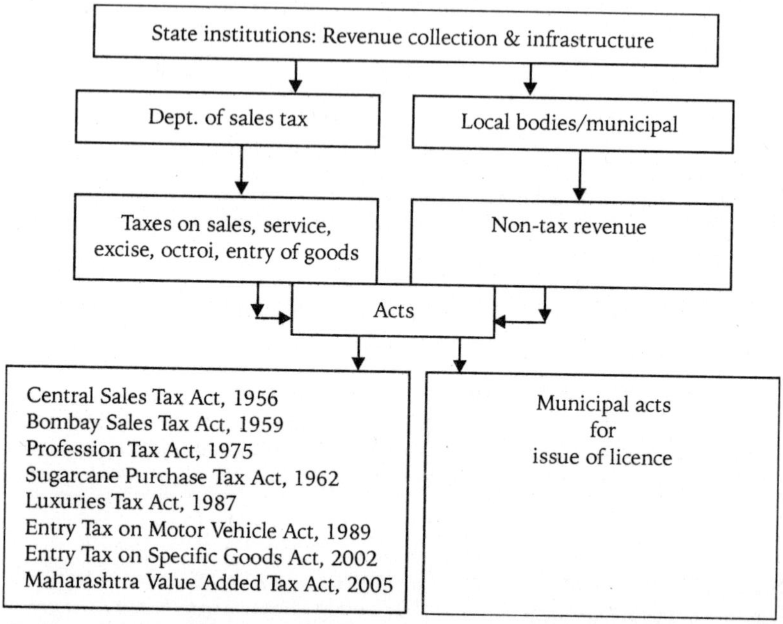

Figure 3.6 maps the state-level institutions involved in policy-making and implementation in Maharashtra in the areas of industries and agriculture.[3]

The Directorate of Industries is a state-level body of industries department that is responsible for implementing government policies for all-round development of industries in the state, with help from different promotional bodies, government departments and agencies. Its primary functions include the following:

- To assist government in formulation of industrial policy, SEZ policy, information technology (IT) policy, biotechnology (BT) policy, package scheme of incentives;
- Implement various promotional schemes, such as citizen charter, registration of IT or BT or ITES (information technology enabled services) or SSI (small scale industries) units;

3. WTO cell established in 2008 is not included in the figure, keeping the reference period in mind.

- Framing of an industrial location policy;
- Grant of licences, permission, recommendation to government of India for Letter of Intent (LoI), IEMs, EOUs, self-employment schemes;
- Raw material assistance to industries;
- Suggests policy measures to state government for all-round industrial development;
- Resolves operational problems by coordinating with inter-department of industries; and
- Provides important statistical information of Maharashtra.

Figure 3.6

State Institutions of Maharashtra in Trade-Related Policies: Industries and Agriculture

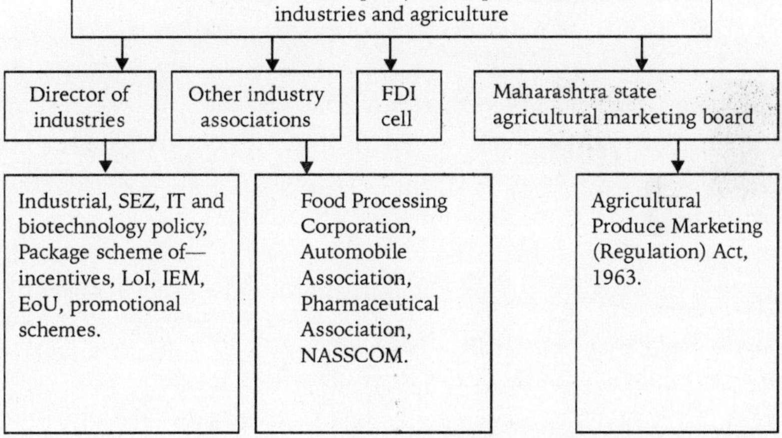

At present, only the director of industries has the broader role of implementing industrial policies and export promotion activities. In absence of any export promotion bureau—such as the one in the state of Uttar Pradesh which is under the department of small scale industry and export promotion—the state of Maharashtra enjoys little power in the making of export policy at the Centre. However, to encourage export activities in the state, it has its own state export awards.[4]

4. Interview with Development Commissioner-Industries, Government of Maharashtra on 9 June 2008, Mumbai.

In the multilateral talks on WTO's agricultural trade, state ruling parties in India continued to showcase the institutionalisation of agricultural subsidy as one of their achievements. India's farmers seemed to have used the state governments as means to pressurise the Centre in favour of cultivators. The states of Karnataka and Kerala have reasonably active WTO cells, which work primarily for their large amount of agricultural products and exports. In Maharashtra, although the talks on establishing a WTO cell have been going on for several years, an active cell was established only in 2008. This cell in Maharashtra consists of representatives from the agriculture and industrial sectors, and some members of the faculty of Indian Institute of Technology (IIT) for consulting, along with representative bodies from industries, such as Confederation of Indian Industries (CII). Representatives from all other sectors are invited in this cell to discuss or recommend their own agenda; the most recent such issue under consideration is for the jewellery sector.[5]

However, WTO cell cannot do anything on implementation of trade policies as that rests with the particular industrial association. For example, Food Processing Corporation, Automobile Association and Pharmaceutical Association assist in implementation of trade policies for their respective industries. But the WTO cell can invite different industry representatives for discussion and submit its recommendations to the respective industry association. Moreover, for the promotion of foreign direct investment (FDI), there is one FDI cell in Maharashtra which works under the department of industries. Its function is to monitor and expedite the FDI proposals.

The next two sub-sections discuss roles of non-institutional players in state-level policies, apart from the above state-level institutions.

Coalition Politics and Political Leadership

The success or failure of implementing any policy in the state is often linked to the political affiliations of the ruling party. It might be driven by the interests of the ruling party of the state or its affiliated party at the Centre (Kennedy, 2004). Sinha (2004a) discusses that the reform initiatives of 1990s at the state level were broadly different across the states as some states like Gujarat took the so-called 'bureaucratic' route, while others like

5. Ibid.

West Bengal, Tamil Nadu and Andhra Pradesh, took 'partisan' strategies. Sinha notes that the coalition government in the state of Tamil Nadu did use its political connection at the Centre in the course of its liberalisation initiative.

The example in Maharashtra's power sector would make even more clear the importance of politics in the making of state-level policy. Since supply of power for agricultural use is highly subsidised in the state, even if the state electricity boards (SEBs) are allowed to decide the power sector tariff freely now, they still need the approval of state governments. In order to ensure its vote banks, the government on the other hand, commits to free or subsidised power supply for their own constituency. Moreover, the inefficiency in usage of irrigation pumps by farmers driven by non-payment of market price adds up to the woes of power suppliers. For a state like Maharashtra with excess supply of power only a few years back, the shortage of power supply—along with the losses incurred by SEBs—has reached a critical stage and needs to be addressed soon.

Several times in history it has happened in India that the multi-party democratic system has allowed the coalition government to rule either the Centre or the state. The formation of coalition government itself is based on a weak foundation of looking at mutual interests over and above the broader benefit of the state. It has been an observed fact that the coalition governments have mostly tried to please their counterpart party in the making of any policies or their implementation (McMillan, 2005: 17-29). If a policy is framed with vested interests in mind, then in the long run, such policy cannot be the most efficient option.

India's political history during the 16 years of liberalisation shows that there was only a single period—that is, 1991-1996—when a single party government ruled the Centre. The economic liberalisation during such period was initiated by the then ruling party government led by the Indian National Congress (INC). Since then, the country has been ruled by a coalition of different parties. In the election of 1996, no party could muster a majority in the Centre, resulting in one of the most difficult times for Indian politics. First, the right wing of Bharatiya Janata Party (BJP) came into power but could not sustain the coalition, hence handing over the power to United Front (UF) government for a short period upto 1998. In 1999, for the first time in Indian history, a non-Congress party and a coalition called National Democratic Alliance (NDA) led by the Prime Minister from BJP completed its full term in the Centre. Finally, another coalition of INC and Communist Party Marxist (CPM), called United Progressive Alliance (UPA) came into power in 2004.

The political scenario in Maharashtra has also been quite similar to that of the Centre, with respect to the volatility of party and coalition politics. Since 1991, there have been several changes in the ruling party at the state level and the leaders of the state. Moreover, the government has mostly been composed of a coalition and not a single party. From 1991 to 1995, two separate chief ministers were sworn in from the same coalition led by the INC. In the next period of 1995 to 1999, the Shiv Sena-BJP coalition government came into power, but again served by two chief ministers, consecutively. Similarly, between 1999 and 2003 and then till date, the coalition named National Democratic Front (NDF) made of Nationalist Congress Party (NCP) and INC has been ruling the state. The INC being the leading party, the chief minister has been elected from them.

Thus, if a comparison is made between the composition of the Centre and that of the state of Maharashtra, it must be noted that from 1991 to 1995, both the ruling parties in the Centre and state were led by the INC even if the latter in state formed a coalition instead of a single party. From 1996 to 1999, the political scenario in both Centre and states has been a little volatile, with both of them having BJP in commanding positions. The major difference between Centre and the state happened during the period of 1999 to 2004, when NDA government came into power as the first non-Congress party in the Centre, but NDF led by INC became the leader in the state.

The present ruling party[6] in the Centre is a coalition of INC (the leading party) and the Left Front, whereas the ruling party in the state is a coalition of INC and NCP. For any policy made at the state level, the latter needs support not only from the leader of INC, but from NCP in the state and from Left parties at the Centre. The Left parties being the most conservative parties in independent India, any reformist policy action at

6. Considering the reference period of 1991-2007, the study avoids discussion of results from the general election of 2009, which again led to the formation of coalition government led by the INC in Centre, leaving the Left parties out this time.

the state level may find it difficult to get through them at the union level. Moreover, to maintain the majority required for ruling the country, the ruling party in Centre at times tries to appease a certain section in the coalition. Hence, they may not always be very supportive to the state chief minister, either. It can be noted that in its present term itself, the chief minister in Maharashtra has been changed twice and already there are discussions going on for bringing back the previous chief minister for a third change.[7] This kind of frequent changes affects decision-making at the state level, particularly, if coalition government rules either state or Centre (Weiner, 1998: 277-93). The conflict between INC, the ruling party in Maharashtra and the opposition of Shiv Sena-BJP coalition over the Dabhol power project, did cost the former dearly in the following election of 1995. The whole project was cut down to only its first phase once Shiv Sena-BJP came into power in the state.

Political instability also discourages investors from coming to the state. Maharashtra had been holding one of the leading positions to the prospective investors since the last two decades with regard to growth in its industrial output, but the instability of leadership in the ruling party prevents the state from taking any major policy decision. The example of one of the largest automobile companies in India based in Maharashtra substantiates the importance of state leadership in trade-related policies and investment in state. The above-mentioned company[8] had earlier signed a MoU with the then chief minister for a project, which would not need any investment from the outside. But when the chief minister was replaced, the project was delayed indefinitely as the company was asked to get the project evaluated by a third party, something which could probably have been avoided if the new chief minister had a stronger say in the cabinet.

Beginning from the year 1991, states have been enjoying more power in their own industrial policies; the more proactive among them are competing among themselves in trying to woo investors through either direct incentives or indirect ones like helping investors improve the economic viability of the unit. Venkatesan and Verma (2000) have

---

7. Keeping the reference period in mind, this study does not discuss the change of chief minister again in the year 2008, right after the 26/11 event in Mumbai.

8. Interview with a senior executive of the company, 5 May and 8 August 2008, Mumbai.

generated an incentive index for a few states of India to compare the incentives they began to offer post-1993 with those in the pre-1993 period. Maharashtra ranks highest in the offer of incentives post-1993. But a survey of managers of several companies in India found that the incentives may indeed help attract investors in the beginning, but in the long term, investors give more importance to the availability of infrastructure, rather than merely the incentives being offered (Venkatesan and Verma, 2000: 49).

Finally, the political economy involved in the government's current SEZ policy and the consequences are recent examples which indicate that the state and the Centre should give enough thought before implementation. Motivated by the desire to compete with China in every aspect, the government announced the SEZ policy in haste. The policy giving private companies relaxations in labour regulations, environmental regulations and tax laws, may distort the competition in the industry, as every industry would like to reach out to one such SEZ zone to remain competitive. Under the SEZ Act, a state can acquire land for industrial purposes only if it involves public interest. The state government of Maharashtra has acquired land in Pen for Reliance and handed over the purchase to the corporate sector, whereas it is still not clear how it has been possible for the state to acquire land without any public interest involved, even before the corporate application has obtained approval from the commerce ministry.

Bureaucratic Systems

Political parties enjoy the power of interfering with the bureaucracy, through say, the transfer of government employee as that power lies with ministers. The Godbole Committee (Godbole, 2001) has presented its report on non-transparency and arbitrary transfer process. If reform could be implemented in Maharashtra's bureaucratic system according to the report, the bureaucracy could be freed from narrow political interests.

The structure of federalism itself can, at times, create problems for reform at the state level. Kumar and Kumar (1996) point out that after the reform policy started in 1991, there were about 19,000 proposals for foreign investment during the period from July 1991 to December 1994, with implementation status of only a few of those. He mentions five major indicators to measure the bureaucratic obstacles in any state of India that the investors should look out for before making their final decision on foreign investment. Those parameters are: power connections; environmental clearance; labour laws; approval for requirements such as land and water; and implementation of regulatory compliance. In the following few paragraphs, the changes in level of bureaucracy in Maharashtra will be explored along these lines.

Power Sector

Government was granted the sole control on ownership and regulation of electricity generation and supply through Electricity (Supply) Act of 1948. The Central Electricity Authority (CEA) at the national level, and the SEBs at the state level, were given the responsibility of generation, transmission and distribution. The power sector being in the concurrent list, it suffered from the conflicts between CEA and the SEBs in implementing the goals during the first few decades. Moreover, uneconomic tariff rate resulting from heavily subsidised industrial supply—compounded by the state government's concern of capturing vote banks—prevented the SEBs from fixing tariff rates and thus recovering from their huge loss. With huge losses and limited capital, along with outdated equipment, Maharashtra did not see any option for the power sector other than inviting private investment (Choukroun, 2002). This development happened in the context of a larger economic crisis that faced India, when the country forced itself to move towards liberalisation, privatisation and globalisation. The US energy company, Enron Corporation, signed a MoU to build a power plant in Dabhol in 1992. From the time of its conception, the project already raised controversies from the point of non-competitive bidding, inefficiency and high tariff rate. Although the first phase was completed by 1999, the project had to be scrapped in 2001 after 95 per cent of its completion. The Enron saga brought foreign investment in the power sector under the scanner.

In 2003, the New Electricity Act was passed, eventually leading to the Maharashtra state government's restructuring of the Maharashtra State Electricity Board (MSEB) in 2005. The restructuring resulted in the formation of four companies. Those are Maharashtra State Power Generation Company Ltd., Maharashtra State Transmission Company Ltd., Maharashtra State Distribution Company Ltd., for power generation, transmission and distribution respectively and the MSEB Holding Co. Ltd.

Up to around 2001-02, Maharashtra was a power surplus state, supplying excess supply to neighbouring states. But after the Enron fiasco blew up and with the industrial and infrastructure development activities starting to expand in the last few years, without any excess generation of power, the power shortage became aggravated. The current power supply shortage in the state is pegged at 4500 MW.

The Electricity Act of 2003 freed power generation from licensing. Captive power generation is free of controls and access is open to captive generation plant subject to availability of transmission facility. Due to concerns for dam safety and inter-state issues, the clearance of CEA for hydro projects is still continuing, but no techno economic clearance (TEC) is required for non-hydro projects. To ensure private sector participation without government guarantee, the distribution companies have been allowed in generation and in turn, the generation companies have been allowed in distribution.

The division of power between Centre and state in the matter of environment policy is not very clear. In general, it seems the Central government is the legislative agency and the state governments are the implementing agencies. With different pollution control acts and political mandates, however, it is the state governments that appear to have enjoyed more power. For environmental clearance to be issued to a new unit, an application for No Objection Certificate (NOC) can be submitted only to the Maharashtra Pollution Control Board (MPCB) after acquiring possession of the land, which may not actually happen for at least one month. Although MPCB has its own sets of standards for different industries, the WTO regime has made industrial bodies more concerned about making their products competitive in the world market. The industry associations themselves are concerned about making their products compatible with world standards in order to get the environmental clearances for international trade. MPCB can thus improve its level of bureaucracy if it works in association with the industry bodies.

Labour Laws

Labour laws being in concurrent list, they are more complicated as both Central and state governments formulate policies, although implementation is done only by the states. The *Doing Business Report* of World Bank

(2006) notes that a typical firm in Maharashtra needs to address 21 different labour-related legislations, a process that becomes time-consuming and costly for those wishing to set up a new venture in the state. At present, 51 different acts define policies regarding labour, wages and units. Some amount of flexibility is available in labour laws under the SEZ Act of 2005, but Maharashtra has not made any significant improvement in this aspect.

Land and Water

The approvals for other requirements such as land and water also need to be issued with adequate efficiency in order to reduce the level of bureaucracy. For example, setting up an industrial unit requires that the proponent deal with somewhere from 12 to 15 various authorities for permissions. The issuance of final clearance from those authorities may take two to three months. After filing an application form, the industrial unit needs to wait for an offer letter, afterwhich it submits an Earnest Money Deposit (EMD). Only then can they expect to receive the issuance letter. After satisfying other requirements, they need the building plans to be approved, as well as water, power connection and NOC from the pollution control board. Assuming that some of these are done simultaneously, the process takes between 30 and 60 days altogether, whereas the Maharashtra Industrial Development Council (MIDC) takes approximately two months to give possession of land to any party interested in setting up industrial units in its jurisdiction.

Changes in Trade-Related Policies and Implementation

This section discusses the change in trade-related policies and the level of implementation in Maharashtra. Since some trade-related policies defined earlier fall within the purview of state industrial policy, a discussion is here made about the major changes in industrial policy, distinct from other changes in trade-related policies for goods and services.

Overall Economic Policy Including Industrial Policy

As a consequence of economic reforms started in 1991, the Maharashtra government set out to break down its controlled regime, the elements of which included its industrial policies, taxation, export-import policies and policies to attract foreign investment. The initial step of state policy supporting liberalisation of 1991 was through simplification of procedures and rationalisation of rules in industries, announced in Industrial Policy of 1993. It has helped the state to expand domestic and international trade and in attracting foreign investment. In support of its efforts towards privatisation, the state government allowed private companies to engage in jetties and minor ports through the build, operate and transfer scheme. The secretary of transport has been designated as the nodal officer for this purpose. In order to seek private participation in power projects, the state government planned to build a mega power plant in Maharashtra.

The state government also realised the need for a prompt response to the changes in global trade policies; that if Maharashtra were to take the most advantage of the emerging opportunities, there must be put in place an effective interface of the government, industry and trade, on a continuous basis. A proposal was then accepted for the constitution of a Board of Industrial and Trade Development under the chairmanship of the chief minister. Similarly, it was decided to empower a Committee of Secretaries on Industrial Development (COSID) under the chairmanship of the chief secretary to ensure the implementation of this policy in a timely manner.

To ensure the higher flow of FDIs, the New Industrial, Trade and Commerce Policy for Maharashtra was announced in 1995 with special importance given to infrastructure development and private sector participation. The new policy was aimed at realigning the government's role from that of a controller to facilitator. It was decided to encourage people to strive for more than merely seeking employment and hone their entrepreneurial skills. The major features of this policy were to support liberalisation along with a thrust on infrastructure in developing regions, private sector participation in developmental efforts, and simplification of procedures and transparency. The comprehensive Information Technology Policy announced in 1998 was planned to help the state in employment generation, along with its effect on industry and trade, financial sector, media and entertainment, health, education and research.

The Industrial Policy of 2001 was specifically targeted to encourage investment in the state. Special capital incentives were designed for small scale industry (SSI) units. It was announced that new SSI units of different areas, including IT and BT units, would be eligible for subsidy of specified rates, to be disbursed in equal annual instalments over five years. Existing SSI and small-scale IT/BT units would be eligible for 75 per cent of the subsidy for expansion, modernisation and diversification, involving additional investment of 25 per cent or more. New industries in C, D and D+ areas[9] and no-industry districts would be exempted from electricity duty for a period of 15 years. Also, for other parts of the state, 100 per cent EOU, IT and BT units, and industries setting up in SEZs and electronic hardware technology parks (EHTP) were exempted from payment of electricity duty for a period of 10 years. IT units in public IT parks were already exempted from stamp duty till March 2006 under the previous industrial policy. The scheme of refund of octroi introduced in the package scheme of incentives in 1993 was extended till March 2006.

Some interest subsidies were also announced for new textile, hosiery and knitwear SSI units. Exemption from sales tax for *khadi* and village industries, financing of capital incentives, and refunds under package scheme were a few other incentives that were handed out. To encourage investment in IT industries, the imposition of turnover tax, additional sales tax, surcharge, or any other additional levy related to sales tax on IT products was suggested to be abandoned, along with the announcement of sales tax at minimum floor rate. Also, floor space index (FSI) was doubled for setting up IT units in IT parks by public bodies.

In the industrial policy of 2006, the exemptions of certain duties were extended in order to slowly move towards compliance with the WTO regime. In C, D, D+ *talukas* and no-industry districts, 100 per cent exemption of stamp duty has been extended till March 2011.

Another way of encouraging investment in the state was through statutory amendment to allow establishment of industrial township in 12 locations across the state. In an attempt to decentralise the control and to make implementation faster, the townships were allowed to raise resources. Between the years 1998 to 2001, the state government also started to

---

9. See the definition of different categories of areas at the MIDC mentioned in the appendix. Source: *http://www.midcindia.org/MIDCWebSite/investment/investscheme.aspx?inav=2*, accessed on 5 June 2009.

develop specialised industrial infrastructure, including IT, BT, leather and chemical. Captive power generation has been permitted to industries throughout the state with respect to IT industries. The Gas Cooperation Agreement between Gas Authority of India Ltd. (GAIL), MIDC and Maharashtra Petroleum Corporation Ltd., would facilitate the planned development of gas supply infrastructure for the industrial fuel supply. Policies were also announced encouraging the development of non-conventional energy.

Development of skilled manpower was also given importance through the provision of land in industrial areas for educational and research institutions of international standards.

Other Trade-Related Policies on Goods and Services

Earlier studies have argued that the major fiscal barrier in inter-state or international trade from the state of Maharashtra appears to be a host of state taxes (NCAER, 2003). Various states with their heterogeneous sales tax structure—topped up by the imposition of a central sales tax (CST), octroi or entry tax—has seen a major hindrance towards creating a common domestic market for several decades. Sales tax being Maharashtra's most important source of revenue over the years, it could not be done away with till the year 2007, even with its negative impacts because of inefficiency in resource allocation. The double taxation, caused by levying taxes on inputs without any set-off, and also on output—along with excise duties—result in cost escalation. These off-set the competitiveness of domestic manufacturing, as getting duty drawback on input taxes for exported goods is more cumbersome.

Octroi also acts as a major impediment to inter-state trade, as it is collected by municipalities during entry of goods in any local area for consumption and sales. Since the rate of octroi is determined and collected by the respective municipal bodies, its rate is quite varied even across different municipal areas. It creates inefficiency in distribution of industries, as industries should ideally be located in places where raw materials are cheaper (Rao and Rao, 2005) instead of based on a few incentives. Different committees have made several recommendations for the complete abolition of this tax, to allow free float in inter-state trade, but the municipal government in Maharashtra has found it difficult to abolish.

The primary reason is the inability to design an alternative source for the same amount of tax revenue, whereas most other states have already abolished it. A few years back, Uttar Pradesh, Gujarat and Rajasthan, have replaced octroi by surcharge on sales tax, and Karnataka and Madhya Pradesh have replaced it with entry tax.

Collection of entry fee of commercial vehicles into their jurisdiction by different states also creates a barrier against inter-state trade, causing distortion in resource allocation because of delays at those checkposts. Additionally, the levy of market fee and cess by state governments on agricultural commodities discourages trading in organised markets.

About government procurement, in India there is no uniform law outlining the procurement policies of government at any level starting from Central to state and local government purchases. The procedures followed by the state governments are restricted by the financial rules of those states, in the same manner that the Centre follows the general financial rules. A few states have the equivalent of Central Store Purchase Organization (CSPO) to monitor the government procurement policy. It is very common with most state governments to give preference to products of the companies arising from its own state in their purchase policy, even accepting the price disadvantage in comparison to procurement from other states. This is usually done to promote the SMEs of the state. There seems to be no clear-cut procurement policy for the government of Maharashtra for its projects. Very recently, the MSMED Act of 2006 clearly mentions in its procurement policy that Central and state governments have to notify their preference policies for procurement of goods and services produced and provided by MSE (medium and small enterprises), by its ministries, department, or its aided institutions and public sector departments.

The Maharashtra Maritime Board (MMB) formed in the year 1996 is in charge of development of port facilities, inland water transport and coastal shipping. The port policy announced by the state of Maharashtra has been looking for private investors to develop minor ports under the build, own operate, share and transfer basis. The company would get a concession period of 50 years, including 5 years for the development, and would raise required capital for development, provide required services, and manage according to the agreement with state government. The

Maharashtra Maritime Board would work as a nodal agency for acquisition of land, development of approach road, and for supply of water. The government has decided to charge Rs. 3 per tonne for the cargo handled in the port, which is supposed to increase in five years, but would not increase to twice the existing tariff. The company would have the full liberty to decide the tariffs for different services. However, for the Central government ports at both Jawaharlal Nehru Port Trust (JNPT) and Mumbai, the Central government decides the tariff rate.

Since standards of infrastructure facilities in a state decide the rate of return on investment and productivity (Babu, 2002; Ghate, 2008), states can do a lot to attract investment through the provision of proper and reliable infrastructure. In the Industrial, Investment and Infrastructure Policy of Maharashtra laid down in 2006, the state is supposed to adopt an innovative cluster development approach to improve its manufacturing competitiveness. Maharashtra Industrial Development Corporation (MIDC) has been given the responsibility of reserving areas for specific industries and land exclusively for SSI or MSI units in and around big industrial areas. The plan of establishing cooperative industrial estates through provision of financial support has also been encouraged. In order to revive the ailing industrial units and close those that have ceased to be viable, the state government has worked out some concession schemes for the former and some waiver of interest for the latter. Also, the weaker units in MIDC areas and cooperative industrial estates willing to exit would be allowed to dispose of their assets, if that land was used either for industrial purpose or for service industries only.

SEZ Policy

Regarding the SEZ policy, the state can primarily select locations, identify partners and recommend those to Centre, along with providing incentives. Maharashtra, contributing to 45 per cent of the country's total exports of goods and services in the country, promptly replied to the SEZ Act of 2001 by passing its own SEZ bill in the same year. The SEZ policy, becoming effective from February 2006, provides 100 per cent exemption from tax, duty and registration, and provides permission for captive power generation. All 100 per cent EOUs would be given the 'public utility service' status with relaxation in labour laws. The resolutions taken at state level in this policy were regarding environment, power supply, water, state taxes, duties, local taxes, labour regulations, SSI or IT registration, law and order, determination of committee on review and development of SEZs.

According to the Maharashtra SEZ Act of 2001, all clearances required from the Maharashtra Pollution Control Board (MPCB) are provided by an empowered committee with a designated development commissioner for that particular SEZ. In this respect, all powers of state governments would be vested only with the development commissioner, who is a Central government employee. The developer of SEZs and other industrial units in that area would be exempted from all types of state taxes for any transaction within the SEZ, or for supply of goods and services from the domestic tariff area to the units or establishments. If any constraints in the system did not allow direct exemption of tax then that would be reimbursed later by the respective authority in the state.

Implementation of Policies in Maharashtra

To support the union trade policy in movement towards liberalisation, the policy instruments do not only lie with the Centre in their customs and excise duties, but the state-level distortions play a major role in preventing the barrier-free trade. A common Indian market can be created through the removal of inter-state differences in tax structure. But the deadline of April 2003 for the implementation of VAT was missed by most of the states, except for Haryana. There was an unsuccessful experiment in Maharashtra in subtraction type VAT from 1995 to 1999. In Maharashtra, although the VAT has been implemented from April 2005, the three tiers of taxes are being continued, including octroi and entry tax.

The following paragraphs discuss other related policies and the status of their implementation.

Industrial Development

To give the desired impetus to the state's industrial development, the New Industrial Policy, 1993 of Maharashtra included a number of provisions like MIDC proposing to establish international industrial parks through FDIs. The government has appointed State Industrial and Investment Corporation of India Ltd. (SICOM) as the nodal agency for coordinating the foreign and NRI investment into the state. In order to expedite the process of clearance in this regard, the state government has proposed to constitute a high-power coordination committee under the chairmanship of the chief secretary, which is mandated to take a prompt decision on such action.

The Industrial, Investment and Infrastructure Policy of Maharashtra, 2006 encourages FDI with the announcement of certain provisions, including the restructuring of industries department, review and monitoring. State government has set up a separate cell, which would work as a single window to handhold for all regulatory affairs and a high-level committee to facilitate a fast-track clearance of all proposals for FDI promotion. The restructuring activities to support the industrial development would include creation of data banks along with computerisation of all departments, staff training and other tasks. It has also been suggested to monitor the implementation of policy decisions at the appropriate level. But the availability of data from industries for monitoring at the state-level implementation of WTO is a problem because the industries are not required to produce such data currently unless they are availing of subsidies or benefits from the state government.[10]

In the same policy, the state government has also announced some packages towards innovative financing and forward-looking, public-private partnership for infrastructure projects such as roads, flyovers, power plants, airports and sea ports. The state had planned for providing a four-lane connectivity in the Mumbai-Pune-Nashik-Aurangabad quadrangle and setting up a special purpose vehicle for that. It has also planned for establishing a natural gas grid and the distribution network in the state; power generation through aggressive public-private ventures; and greater recognition and incentives to energy conservation and non-conventional energy initiatives. It was also proposed to set up a committee under the chairmanship of the chief secretary with members from concerned departments for resolution of infrastructure issues concerning industries. Two new international airports have been planned, one in Chakan near Pune, and another in Navi Mumbai, along with a multi-modal international air-cargo and passenger hub in Nagpur. However, none of these airports have begun construction. Seven more ports have been planned in the state and some of those are in the making. Industrial

10. For further discussion on sub-national differences in policies, and their implementations to attract FDI in the state, see Saez (2002).

clusters have been developed at Nashik, Kolhapur, Nagpur and Aurangabad. A Delhi-Mumbai industrial corridor has been linked up to Delhi-Mumbai freight corridor to attract investors.

One noticeable move forward in this respect is the Maharashtra Airport Development Company's focused initiative for the development of greenfield airports in Shirdi, Jalgaon, Sholapur, Chandrapur and Dariya. The government is also planning to take care of infrastructure bottlenecks in minor ports through highway and railway connectivity. State government is doing some kind of transport facility study to solve this connectivity issue, particularly to tackle the fast expansion of industries in the Pune region. It has been suggested by the MIDC that in the coming decades, availability of water in the growing industrial areas might be a problem and in order to tackle that, industries would probably need to pay more for recycling of water as the dams have been fully used. This one is being considered by MIDC recently as a development rule.

Customs Administration

State officials, even prior to liberalisation, have already been given the mandate of imposing penalties on those found violating customs regulations. The state has kept such mandate, post-liberalisation, but they still do not clear goods. After liberalisation, the government has slowly reduced the number of different classifications and rates for customs to make it even simpler. But it still takes at least two days for clearance, and one reason for such delay is the complex structure of classification. Since Maharashtra has a few of the country's major ports, it has an indirect role in improving the customs administration in order to help international trade. The state-level incentives and tax refund also make things a little complicated at times.

Power Sector

Maharashtra has the highest installed capacity among all states, including both public and private power generation; it also has the largest demand. In Mumbai area, there are three public utility companies supplying power, and outside Mumbai, Maharashtra State Electricity Board (MSEB) is the sole supplier. As the power sector has not been developed yet to face the open competition, the budgetary support to this sector—which includes subsidy

that would have affected the century-old profession of a large coastal population.

In absence of any reform in the old Land Acquisition Act, 1894, the farmland converted to a modern township over 400 acres of land at Magarpatta near Pune has been taken on lease from the farmers instead of acquiring, which gives farmers an ownership after the development. It has sustained the farmers' right to cultivate the land after the contract date and the land has been used by the software companies, along with building of schools, malls and hospitals. This kind of transformation may be a better proposition, as it does not take away the private land forcefully; rather the farmers gave away for lease willingly. The Urban Land Ceiling act and Rent Control act in the state seem to be outdated and reduce the flow of FDI, even in the real estate sector. More recently, the Maharashtra government made some proactive moves in this respect, repealing the Urban Land Ceiling Act to increase the FSI.

In a recent seminar in Mumbai,[11] one MIDC executive presented the fact that the Maharashtra government has been able to acquire about 10,000 acres of land in the last two years, with consent, under the Land Acquisition Act, 1894, which is probably an indication that the government in its own initiative can significantly resolve the land acquisition issues. The recent initiatives of MIDC through international biotech park at Hinjawadi, biotech park at Jalna, specialised food park at Butibori, silver zone at Hupri, grape processing parks at Vinchur and Palus, floriculture park at Talegaon, textile parks at Butibori and Ambarnath, and gems and jewellery park at SEEPZ, are improving the state's industrial infrastructure and helping trade and business in Maharashtra.[12]

Concluding Note

This chapter sought to examine the performance of Maharashtra in policy-making and implementation, from the beginning of the economic reform till 2007, in areas related to international trade. In the course of its discussion, the chapter described the roles being played by different state

11. Seminar on *Export Competitiveness of Maharashtra* held on 12 August 2008 at WTC, as a joint collaboration between WTC and MEDC.

12. WTC Research Study on *Export Competitiveness of Maharashtra*, August 2008.

institutions, as well as non-institutional factors. Among the institutional factors, some of the tax reforms are in the purview of state and local bodies. Maharashtra has not been very forward in its tax reform, particularly regarding octroi, else it would reduce trade distorting tax and would prevent movement of existing investment outside the state.

The state-level institutions, such as director of industries, have been proactive in making its industrial policies suitable to attract investors with provision of several incentives. But the sustainability of attracting investment through incentives—as compared to the way of developing infrastructure—does not get much support from the industrial houses in the long run. The state has developed several specific industrial belts and some SEZs to support industry and trade. Maharashtra Economic Development Council (MEDC) is another such body, which identifies areas for improvement and proposes the state government for policy changes and implementation. It invites industrial bodies to participate in the making of proposals.

Although the state of Maharashtra has been able to attract investors through its incentives, schemes and cluster development initiatives, the competition with other states calls for more sustainable initiatives, such as the development of reliable infrastructure. Development of port facility and uninterrupted power supply seem to be two major issues in this respect.

Among other non-institutional factors, existing literature have identified state-level leadership and party politics as major determinants in reform. Maharashtra cannot showcase its leadership in reform process like the states of Andhra Pradesh or Gujarat. Moreover, the instability in state politics affected the desired growth of power sector in the state. The recent sloppiness in state power sector is perhaps a fine example in support of the argument for transparency in state bureaucracy and the need for it to be freed from political interest of leading parties for ensuring uninterrupted power supply.

Finally, the initiatives at the government level need to be in coordination with the requirements of the industry. Once the WTO cell starts working actively in Maharashtra, it will probably help the state more to identify areas of improvement in trade and industry.

4 Economic Performance of Maharashtra

Introduction

This chapter puts the spotlight on certain indicators that will help summarise Maharashtra's overall economic performance after liberalisation was set in motion. The purpose is to understand the ability of Maharashtra to reflect its liberalisation initiative on its overall performance and to understand the future prospects for the state. Infrastructure being a major area contributing to expansion of international trade and investment as discussed earlier, a section of this chapter discusses in more detail the state's performance in that area. The chapter is organised as follows:

- Section II discusses the performance of the state in terms of few macroeconomic indicators, such as growth indicators, patterns of revenue receipts, patterns of state financing, some other regulatory and governance indicators and availability of physical infrastructure in the state.
- Section III attempts to answer the question of whether or not Maharashtra has been able to take advantage of the liberalisation initiative, by looking into the size of government and the regulations on labour, credit and business.
- Section IV gives a summary of the effects of liberalisation on trade and industry in the state.
- Section V concludes the chapter.

Macroeconomic Indicators in the State

Growth Indicators

According to the *State Development Report* of 2005, Maharashtra's growth in state domestic product during 1992-1997 has been the second highest in the country at 8.9 per cent, after the 12.4 per cent of Gujarat. In the 1997-2002 period, however, Maharashtra's rate of domestic product growth declined to 4.7 per cent, placing the state at seventh position. The Tenth Plan (2002-2007) target has been estimated at 7.4 per cent, but lagging behind the growth rate of eight states. However, the state economy has been growing at an average of 9.4 per cent in 2006-07 and Maharashtra ranks number one in state domestic product accounting, which is over 13 per cent of the national GDP. The state's contribution to national fiscal receipts is over 40 per cent and the literacy rate is above 77 per cent.

Pattern of Revenue Receipts in States

If we look at the pattern of revenue receipts in the state over the period from 1985-86 to 2005-06, we can see that amount of revenue receipts has been increasing but the rate of increase has not been same in all those years. Revenue increases at a lower rate initially but later, the rate of increase in revenue speeds up. That is, it was increasing at almost the same rate up to 1990-91, and then the rate of increase in revenue increased from 1991-92 and continued with the same speed up to 1997-98. Again that rate increases from 1998-99 and kept increasing almost at the same rate up to the year 2004-05. These revenue receipts include tax receipts and non-tax receipts, where tax receipts include state taxes and share in central taxes; and non-tax receipts include interest receipts and grants from the Centre.

Figure 4.1

Revenue Receipts by Maharashtra

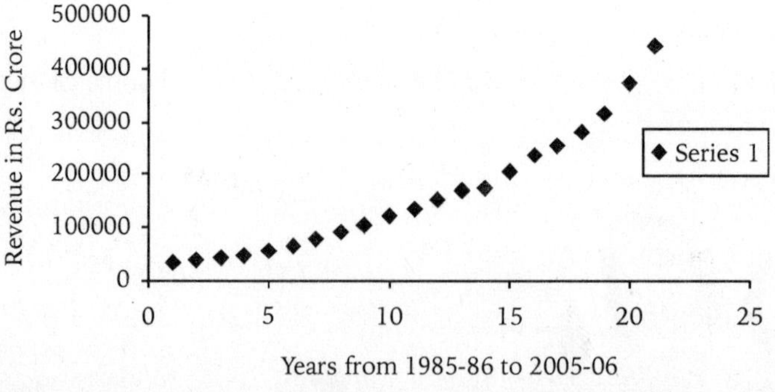

Source: Table on Pattern of Receipts of the State Governments, taken from Budget documents of state government from RBI.

Further details of the components of state tax receipts reveal that throughout all these years, the share of sales tax in this tax receipt has been around 40 per cent, while that of state excise duty has been approximately 11 per cent. This implies as and when sales, internal trade or collection of taxes by the state from other sources has increased in Maharashtra. Both the above tax rates have been reduced only up to that extent to maintain the same share in the basket of total state tax collection.

Pattern of State Financing

In order to look at the pattern of state financing, we should also find out what other receipts the state received over the years and the general pattern or trend of those receipts. Except for the revenue receipts as earlier explained, the state received capital receipts, which include public accounts on a net basis. Therefore, the total receipts comprised revenue receipts and capital receipts has increased, following the same trend of increasing the revenue receipts as explained in the previous section.

On the overall state financing, Maharashtra had to resort to borrowings to meet the increasing expenditures over and above the receipts. The total debt as a ratio of GSDP of government of Maharashtra has increased from 14 per cent in 1993-94 to 25 per cent in 2004-05. This total debt includes the public debt, borrowings from small savings and provident funds, interest obligations on other borrowings. In addition to these, there has been an increasing amount of off-budget borrowings through creating of special purpose vehicles (SPVs). According to Pethe and Lalvani (2005), most of the money borrowed through SPVs have been put into irrigation projects and haven't been used properly. Therefore, they suggest public-private partnership as a better option than borrowing through SPVs for infrastructure projects as there is a chance of inefficient use in the latter.

Governance and Institutional, Regulatory, Quality Indicators

The basic idea behind economic reform accompanied by a liberalised trade regime was to open the economy to foreign investors by allowing them the option of free trade and in turn, India should get the advantage of the same. This whole idea of growth with the help of foreign investment was based on the premise of good governance. State governments have an important role in ensuring good governance through an efficient and reliable legal system, physical infrastructure, basic health, education, civic amenities and a social safety net. Hence, there seems to exist a strong relationship between good governance and private investment in the states.

Maharashtra being one of the most industrialised States in India, along with the presence of Mumbai, the financial capital of the country, it is perceived as a 'badly administered' state too. The primary reason—as noted in the *State Development Report* for Maharashtra (2005)—is that while pursuing its economic goals, the state fails to look after the welfare of its under-privileged population. The benefits of access to education, employment and health have not trickled down to the poor. According to the *National Human Development Report* of 2001, Maharashtra ranked fourth among 15 major states of the country in human development index (HDI).

Meanwhile, in the Index for Social and Economic Infrastructure, the state ranked sixth behind the states of Punjab, Kerala, Tamil Nadu, Haryana and Gujarat. This index took into account the states' economic competitiveness and the presence of certain social infrastructures. The rank of Maharashtra has been declining over the previous few years, as the growth in economic social infrastructure has not been equitable across all population groups of the state.

In order to recover from the acute fiscal stress faced by the state at the tail-end of the 1990s, the government adopted a medium-term fiscal reforms programme beginning December 2001. It was expected to further improve the fiscal discipline, and in view of that, the Maharashtra Fiscal Responsibility and Budgetary Management (FRBM) Act was passed in April 2005.

Availability of Physical Infrastructure

Maharashtra is the third largest state in India in terms of land area. It has one of the best road networks across the country, with the Maharashtra State Road Transport Corporation (MSRTC) as well as private operators providing connectivity. The total length of roads is 2,29,302 km, with 4,176 km of national highways and 33,705 km of state highways.[1] The

1. India Brand Equity Foundation (2008).

ongoing National Highways Development Project (NHDP) is aimed at upgrading 721 km of roads into four six-lane highways; of this total, 319 km has been done. Some other highway upgradation schemes are also undergoing with an additional length of about 611 km.

The state capital, Mumbai, is one of the country's major hubs in railway network. It has three major stations and headquarters of two railway zones. According to a 2008 study of the Indian Brand Equity Foundation, Mumbai's suburban railway transports an estimated 6.1 million local passengers everyday on its intra-city network. The city is home to India's busiest airport, along with three more airports in the cities of Pune, Nagpur and Nashik. The state's airport handles 34 per cent of the country's international passengers. One more airport is being planned near Navi Mumbai and another Greenfield airport is to be built near Pune.

Maharashtra's two major ports are the Mumbai port and Nhava Sheva. Mumbai port, situated in the west coast of India, is a natural harbour. It handles cargo of all types, accounting for a sixth of the entire sea-borne trade of the country. Out of its total port traffic, 44 per cent originates from Maharashtra itself, and Mumbai accounts for 28 per cent of the total traffic. The entire port is served by an extensive railway network connected to the central and western railways and a road network of 126 km in length.

The Container Corporation of India Ltd. (CONCOR) was incorporated in 1988 under the Companies Act and started its operations from 1989, after it took over the then existing network of seven ICDs from the Indian Railways. Its primary functions involved providing inland transport for containers by rail, management of ports, air cargo complexes and establishment of cold chain. Rail link plays the most important role in decongesting ports and road corridors, thus the majority of CONCOR terminals are rail-linked. It also has a network of 57 terminals, and some more facilities such as warehousing, container parking, repair facilities and office complexes.

Also, India's first fully computerised and automated airport, Jawaharlal Nehru Port Trust (JNPT) was commissioned in Maharashtra in 1989. The port helps in domestic and international trade to other neighbouring states, such as Karnataka, Gujarat and Madhya Pradesh. The container terminal of this port has three berths, with a total current capacity of 6 lakh TEUs per year. It has good connectivity to ICDs and serves the needs of the existing 13 container freight stations (CFSs). It is expected to soon serve 9 more CFS. The private container terminal, Nhava Sheva International Container Terminal, also serves the ports.

Future plans for expansion include extension of container berth to handle extra container traffic, faster turnaround time, and the provision of accommodation for large container vessels. This includes construction of a 50m-long finger jetty, planned to start operations by 2008.[2]

Since JNPT is connected to the national rail network through Panvel-Uran line of central railway, the port's capacity to handle trains has been planned to be increased from 12 to 18 trains per day each way. Also, the primary road connectivity of the port at present is through the national highway (NH-4B) to Mumbai-Pune expressway, Mumbai-Goa Highway (NH-17) and through a two-lane state highway (SH-54) to Navi Mumbai, Thane, Nashik and Ahmedabad. A SPV between JNPT, National Highway Authority of India (NHAI) and CIDCO has been set up to improve road connectivity to meet the growing amount of container traffic. To improve the port's internal road connectivity for handling increased container traffic, the port is widening its existing roads from four lanes to six or eight lanes, along with the development of parking areas at various locations. Mumbai Port Trust has also taken up a proposal for the construction of two offshore container berths for handling vessels of 6000 TEU capacities. Once this is implemented, Mumbai Port's cargo handling capacity will increase by 10 million tonnes per annum.

The Delhi-Mumbai industrial corridor, which is in the developing stage, is a key opportunity to attract investors in the state as well as promote internal and external trade from Maharashtra. The total length of the corridor is 1,483 km, of which Maharashtra has a share too.

Maharashtra has the largest installed electricity generation capacity in the country. Between 1990-91 and 2002-03, its capacity increased from 8,876 MW to 15,152 MW. In 1991-92 and 2001-02, it was ranked fourth in all of India in terms of per capita capital availability.

---

2. *Source: WTC Research Study on Export Competitiveness of Maharashtra*, 2008.

Were the Policies Geared to Taking Advantage of the Economic Liberalisation or Were they Protective in Nature?

It is imperative that a state allowing larger economic freedom to its citizens move faster to take advantage of liberalisation policy. Debroy and Bhandari (2005) has identified three broad categories to measure the economic freedom of states, namely: size of government measured by expenditures, taxes and enterprises; regulation of credit, labour and business and legal structure; and security of property rights. These authors have developed indices for the above three categories, along with a composite index, to compare performance across states. According to this study, Maharashtra has slipped down in its composite index rank, from sixth position in 2004 to tenth in 2005.

In the following sections, we will analyse some of the indicators from the first two categories, which are relevant to trade policies at the state level, and examine how Maharashtra has faired in taking advantage of liberalisation while framing its trade policies.

Size of Government Measured by Expenditures, Taxes and Enterprises

In this study, the indicators of the size of government is considered in a manner that a larger size would mean higher interference in business and economic activities by government. In this overall category, Maharashtra has gone down from ninth position in 2004 to fourth in 2005. However, in an attempt to reduce government interference in the power sector, the state has been trying to change the power subsidy over the years. Table 4.1 gives an idea about the state's initiative in that respect.

Total revenues from taxes on property and capital transactions as a ratio of GSDP are much higher in this state.

As the Central government has announced its target of bringing down state revenue deficit to zero by the year 2008-09, the Maharashtra state government has started to work towards such goal through increasing its tax revenue and controlling revenue expenditure. Also, with the reduction of non-tax receipts by the state over the years, the burden of fiscal corrections has been on the state tax revenues. Therefore, the state government has announced measures to increase tax-GSDP ratio. The tax revenue to GSDP percentage has decreased from 9.43 per cent to 8.36 per cent from 2000-01 to 2002-03, even if the absolute figure in collection of tax revenue increased between the years. But the percentage has again increased to 8.70 per cent and 9.20 per cent in 2003-04 and 2004-05, respectively.

Table 4.1

Changes in the Amount of Power Subsidy by State Electricity Boards

	Power Subsidy (Rs. Cr.)	*Capital Outlay and Net Lending (Rs. Cr.)*	*Budgetary Support to Power Sector (Rs. Cr.)*
	(1)	*(2)*	*(3) = 1+2*
1993-94	0	450	450
1994-95	0	730	730
1995-96	0	350	350
1996-97	0	760	760
1997-98	0	690	690
1998-99	0	510	510
1999-2000	0	450	450
2000-01	2371	220	2591
2001-02	629	719	1348
2002-03	712	439	1151
2003-04 (RE)	835	287	1122
2004-05 (BE)	713	161	874

Source: Table A: 11 of Pethe and Lalvani (2005).

At the actual level of implementation, with the help of the Maharashtra Single Window Clearance and Industrial Facilitation Act of 2006, the state government is trying to create a single window clearance system for any party interested in setting up industries in the state. MIDC being the body providing infrastructure facilities for small, medium and large enterprises to be set up in the MIDC areas, it needs to give all types of permissions, clearances and approvals required in setting up any industrial unit in its jurisdiction. It has already launched an e-governance initiative, beginning with the acceptance of online applications for the allotment of land. The interested party needs to submit online its application in common application form (CAF) format and is given 10 days to submit all required documents. At present, the process does not cover any other permission, and MIDC is working towards having it soon expanded to other areas.

Since implementation of regulatory compliance falls in the concurrent list, it implies that if a company has to comply with six different laws enacted by the Central government, then six different inspectors must check such compliance before issuing a final approval. This again lengthens the bureaucracy and becomes a discouraging factor for investment.

To address this issue and support the states' initiative for single window clearance, some initiatives have recently been launched at the Union government level. As a pilot, they have selected a number of locations in several states and are working on the identification of services that need to be taken in this single window clearance system. It has asked the Maharashtra government to provide necessary details about the required permissions and approvals for setting up industries in the state. Once the single window clearance system starts at the Central level, it will be coordinated with state-level requirements. For example, the clearance required from the tax authorities and all such requirements under union jurisdiction, will slowly be integrated into the state-level system and be made as a unique single window clearance system for industries.

While the stamp duty and registration is the most important source of state tax, the reduction in the rates has proven to help the state in terms of improved compliance and realisation of duty. The government has committed in its Fiscal Policy Strategy for Maharashtra 2006-07, to "reduce and rationalise" the stamp duty rates in other segments and transactions.

Regulation of Credit, Labour and Business

A state is supposed to enjoy higher economic freedom if its business houses enjoy larger control on labour along with availability of infrastructure, and has fewer constraints in terms of cost in carrying trade and other economic activities. Maharashtra has moved down in this category from being in the top position in 2004 to sixth in 2005. The following section will discuss the impact of liberalisation policies in Maharashtra, analysing the indicators that are relevant to the state's trade policies.

Number of Special Economic Zones

Setting up of SEZs encourages more economic and trade-related activities as that comes with tax breaks with minimum regulations from government. Maharashtra still needs to increase this number as compared to some forerunners, such as Gujarat, UP, TN, WB and Kerala. An estimate of the number of SEZs in different states as of May 2008 shows that Maharashtra stands seventh out of 10 states with 27, whereas Andhra Pradesh has the highest at 54 SEZs.[3]

Minimum Licence Fee for Traders

Maharashtra has minimum licence fee for traders as compared to other states, which implies more economic freedom to traders.

Power Shortage as a Percentage of Total Demand

Maharashtra has a very high rate of power shortages during peak working hours, which indicates less freedom and less productivity for business houses.

Labour Laws and Procedures

Under the Industry, Investment and Infrastructure Policy of 2006, the state government has initiated reforms in labour laws to create a legislative framework conducive to facilitate industries and investment. The provisions under the new policy include the following:

- Working hours to be increased to 60 hours a day from 48 hours;
- Termination of workers is to be permitted under the condition of payment of adequate compensation;
- Female workers to be allowed to work in night shift and also for 12-hour periods;
- Amendments in some sections of Industrial Disputes Act, 1947 in order to provide flexibility to the units that are supposed to be affected by flexibility of market demand and changes in technology and global competition.

3. *Source:* MEDC, 2008.

Also, recently introduced self-certification process and the reduction in the number of documents to be registered and maintained is a step forward towards reform of labour laws.

The state government has taken initiatives to restructure labour laws that would remove disincentives to additional employment generation, facilitate restructuring and technological upgradation, in the context of global competition. It has proposed to set up a committee that comprises representatives from industries and labour to review the Maharashtra Recognition of Trade Union and Prevention of Unfair Labour Practices Act. It was also proposed to reduce the lengthy paper work required for industrial units. The then 46 registers, forms and returns required from various industrial establishments have been either clubbed or substituted or deleted altogether.

What has been the Effect of these Liberalisation Policies on Trade and Industry in the State?

In a democratic federation like India, the state-level industries department has roles primarily on the framing of policies. State can set their goals and identify sectors accordingly for further development. It can frame its industrial policies accordingly. For example, Maharashtra identified IT and BT sectors, which might need separate policy framework and acted accordingly. After the framing of industrial policy, the industries department can, at the maximum send instructions to its own department. But it cannot ensure that all other departments would follow the same objective. The industries department cannot ask defence department or agricultural or ministry of power to frame their policies accordingly to help the industries develop in the state. That has to be done only at the chief ministerial level. If the state's chief minister understands the importance of industries then he can call higher authorities of all departments and ask them to follow the same objective.

The host of taxes and incentives increases the bureaucracy's discretionary power. The CAF, if introduced, will reduce personal contact with bureaucracy for all official matters, and in turn will increase transparency and reduce corruption. But it is all still at the initial stages in

Maharashtra. As mentioned by some executives of MEDC in a seminar[4] that Bajaj Auto has recently shifted their location out of Akrudi due to the octroi level in the state; the state government needs to take care of this trade-distorting tax.

If transparency and accountability is not imposed and maintained then it is better to reduce those inefficient ways of promoting industries through incentives and spend that amount in developing activities, such as infrastructure build-up, construction of major ports and airports and increasing connectivity among them through roads and proper transports.

Private sector participation in infrastructure development is the need of the hour. In this, the Electricity Act of 2003 should be viewed as the pioneer and model. But the cross-subsidisation, as mentioned earlier, may again upset the benefit of industries.

If investors lose money due to delay in turnaround time at ports and airports, then they will definitely choose to move to other countries. Comparing the volumes of traffic among India's major 12 ports, it will be noted that the commodity-wise traffic was highest at the Mumbai port in 1990-91, whereas it was lowest in JNPT.[5] By 2001-02, the traffic in Mumbai port has dropped from a figure of 28,899 thousand tonnes to 15,865 thousand tonnes, but the traffic at JNPT has increased from 2,022 thousand tonnes to 13,120 thousand tonnes in the same reference period, and moved up to sixth position from the lowest one. The amount of goods going through JNPT of Maharashtra accounts for 60 per cent of the total cargo in the country, so the state has a bigger responsibility to construct another major port and reduce the burden of JNPT. Moreover, JNPT being located at one corner of the country, the travel time and cost is also higher when goods from all over the country needs to reach there. Currently, the maritime board is planning to construct another port facility and connect that with other parts of the state through a road network, potentially reducing the JNPT congestion and facilitating trade from the state and the country.

With the MSMED Act of 2006, the process of two-stage registration of micro and small enterprises has been replaced with filling of memoranda

4. Seminar on *Export Competitiveness of Maharashtra* held on 12 August 2008 at WTC, as a joint collaboration between WTC and MEDC.

5. MEDC (2002a), p.67, Table VU.

and it is made optional for service sector medium enterprises, small and micro enterprises. Thus, collecting data from these industries at the state level for monitoring the progress becomes difficult. The industries taking advantage of government schemes and incentives are only mandated to register; it is the industries department that has the responsibility of collecting data from them.

Concluding Note

The 2001 census puts the count of Maharashtra's population at 9.69 crore; the number was projected to increase to 10.80 crore by March 2008. The literacy rate in the state, according to the same census, is 76.9 per cent, with 86 per cent and 67 per cent for males and females, respectively. But the July 2007-June 2008 NSS 64th Round shows that the rate has increased to 86.2 and 69.3 per cent, respectively, for males and females.

The 2007-08 Economic Survey of Maharashtra notes that from the beginning of liberalisation till July 2007, 3,982 FDI projects were approved by the Government of India, with an investment of Rs. 70,856 crore in this state. Some 1,623 of these projects have been commissioned up to July 2007, which is about 55 per cent of the total approved value. Following is the breakdown of these approved FDI projects: services (24 per cent); IT (21 per cent); infrastructure (12 per cent); and automobiles (10 per cent). The total road length maintained by the PWD and ZPs in Maharashtra as of March 2007 was 2.34 lakh km, and total rail route length is 5,902 km which is about 9.2 per cent of the total rail route length of the country. The total number of motor vehicles on the road of Maharashtra as of January 2008 is 130.3 lakh. As the same economic survey notes, that the service sector is the largest contributor to the GSDP, investment in infrastructure will have a big impact on the state GSDP. This can only be done through a larger number of public-private partnership (PPP) investments. Maharashtra has been one of the forerunner states in taking up PPP projects, particularly in infrastructure, which is directly linked to the performance of external sector. The primary issue that remains to be addressed, therefore, is not the direction taken to support the liberalisation but perhaps the efficiency of actions.

5 Case Studies

CASE STUDY I: AUTOMOBILE AND AUTO COMPONENTS INDUSTRY

Introduction

The liberalisation polices of the Government of India was announced in 1991 and consequently, the economy was thrown open to foreign players. Till then, the country's automobile industry was controlled by a strict policy regime, which prevented competition from outside. With competition being mild, there was no need for technological improvement, research and development, and investment. But the economic liberalisation helped the multinational companies (MNCs) like Ford, Toyota, Hyundai, Honda, DaimlerChrysler, Peugeot, Daewoo, Mercedes Benz and General Motors, to expand their operations in India (Narayanan and Vashisht, 2008; MVIRDC World Trade Centre, 2005). This expansion helped the Indian auto component industry to grow further with the help of foreign collaboration. As the local manufacturers were unable to keep up with the demand of global players in terms of technology, size, along with the costly imports of components, the international manufacturers pressurised their existing suppliers to expand in India. Delphi, following the General Motors, set up a facility in Gujarat in 1995; Visteon later did the same. Also, the domestic players in auto and auto components industry began engaging in technical collaborations with globally acclaimed manufacturers, except for the few low-end products like casting, brake linings, sheet metals, pistons and piston rings.

Only after the first phase of liberalisation initiatives of Government of India, the growth of automobile sector in India has been as steep as 22 per cent between the years 1992 to 1997.[1] The exports of commercial vehicles

1. *Source:* Automotive Components Manufacturers Association of India, "Industry Statistics", *http://www.acmainfo.com/*, accessed on 6 June 2009.

have increased at a Compound Annual Growth Rate (CAGR) of 1.3 per cent, the exports in the passenger car segment increased at a CAGR of 20.2 per cent and exports in the two-wheeler segment increased at a CAGR 11.1 per cent during the same reference period. The import of automobiles also increased during this period and it was as high as Rs. 447 crore in 2003.

Along with the automobile sector, the auto component sector is also regarded as a highly competitive segment among the manufacturing industries in India after the economic liberalisation. This sector grew fast primarily due to its demand for exports. This sector has maintained about 10 to 12 per cent of exports out of its total production. In 2007, the auto component sector in India emerged as the highest growing sector with a growth rate of 21 per cent in the year. It crossed a total turnover of Rs. 64,500 crore with exports of Rs. 12,643 crore. Today, India is looked upon as a major outsourcing hub of automobile parts for multinational companies like Ford, General Motors, DaimlerChrysler, Fiat, Volkswagen and Toyota, to name a few.

The opening up of the automotive sector to the foreign investors has increased the amount of investment in this sector from Rs. 50,000 crore in the year 2002-03 to Rs. 80,000 crore in the year 2007. A recent MEDC (Maharashtra Economic Development Council) report (MEDC, 2008) shows that the automobile sector in Maharashtra only has received about Rs. 895 crore of foreign direct investment (FDI).

There are several studies (MVIRDC World Trade Centre, 2005: 58-65; Okada, 1998; Sutton, 2004) about the impact of India's liberalisation policies on the Indian automobile industry or auto component industry. But to my knowledge, there is no important contribution in literature investigating the growth of this industry in the state of Maharashtra and initiatives of the state government, in light of the liberalisation policy. This particular study intends to explore how the automobile and auto components industry of Maharashtra has been able to use the liberalisation policies in its favour from the year 1991 onwards. The scope of the study is limited between the years of 1991 to 2007.

The study finds that Maharashtra has been one of the frontrunners in development of automobile and auto components industry in the last more than one decade due to the huge presence of forward and backward linkages. Different schemes of the state government for development of industrial clusters have helped the state to attract foreign and domestic investments over the years. The study establishes that the availability of incentives seems to be one decisive factor in determining investment destinations of industrial companies. But for attracting investors in the State other factors are equally important, such as availability of infrastructure like port connectivity, uninterrupted power supply, as well as skilled manpower (*State Development Report of Maharashtra*, 2005). These are the areas of development that the state should concentrate on for the sustainable development of industry. The improvement of port facility—according to the nature of this industry—such as vehicle parking and maintenance facility at port would contribute to higher internal and international trade. The other important areas in which the state has roles to play are the unification of tax structure across states, and faster processing of its reimbursement schemes.

The next few sections are arranged as follows:

- Section II discusses the union trade policy for the automotive sector during the reference period and the structure of the industry in India.
- Section III deals with state-level policy and implementation initiatives for this sector in Maharashtra. The two parts of this section constitute the trends of development of the automotive industry in Maharashtra, the role of the state government in that process and the initiatives of Maharashtra in policy implementations.
- Section IV explores the recent initiatives of the state in light of bureaucracy and recent concerns of the industry along with implementation issues.
- Section V concludes the study with some policy implications.

Union Trade Policy Related to this Sector

The economic liberalisation of the 1990s initiated the delicensing of automobile industry. In 1993, the government started eliminating licences, encouraging the setting up of 16 new manufacturers of cars in the country. The delicensing of the passenger car segment in 1993 helped the international players to enter. The trade policy allowed the import of technology with a royalty payment of 5 per cent without any duration limit for production of passenger cars. The removal of quantitative restrictions on automobile imports and the progressive liberalisation of the norms of foreign investment—making it permissible up to 100 per cent in automatic route—are major liberalisation policies as well.

Finally, the financial liberalisation supported through expansion of credit facilities raised the demand for automobile, and created a large market in the country itself.[2]

The Ministry of Heavy Industries, Government of India, announced its Auto Policy in 2002 (Government of India Auto Policy, 2002), which targets to establish a globally competitive automotive industry in India, and 'to double its contribution to economy by 2010'. This policy helped to reduce duties in the auto component sector to a large extent, and automobile sector to some extent, along with supporting R&D initiatives. The implementation of VAT in a few states in 2005-06 was also a major motivator for the industry. Finally, the Euro III emission norms introduced in 11 metro cities and Euro II norms in the rest of the cities in 2005-06, was a major initiative to make the industry globally competitive.

The Indian automobile components industry supplies to two types of clients, namely, original equipment manufacturers (OEMs) and replacement buyers. This industry can be divided into three categories: under the first one falls the MNCs like Delphi or Visteon, who function through wholly owned subsidiaries or the ones like Denso India, MICO who works through units in which they have the control; the second ones are the Indian companies with foreign collaborations such as Indian Nippon Electricals, IP Rings and Wheels India; and the third category includes companies like Sundaram Brake Linings and Sundaram Fasteners, who have no or minimum foreign collaboration. The liberalisation policy of the government has brought a structural change in the Indian automotive sector in the last more than a decade, where the supply chain is such that the small components are usually supplied to the system integrators, instead of the vehicle manufacturers. This has created a huge opportunity

2. For further details on trade policy for the automotive sector, see the website link to *International Trade Policy Issues* in Society for Indian Automobile Manufacturers: *http://www.siamindia.com/* accessed on 5 June 2009.

for the small-scale industrial units to be tier one and tier two manufacturers. They supply the small components to the tier one companies, usually large companies or MNCs, who in turn supply the components to the vehicle manufacturers. The liberalisation policy of 1991, allowing entry of global OEMs and tier one suppliers in India, actually helped the expansion of auto component manufacturers.

About 85 per cent of the auto component requirements by the Indian industries are met through domestic industry and only 15 per cent are imported. The primary reason of imports of auto components is that certain auto components are not produced in India, or some of them being limited in demand, are not cost-effective to produce domestically. Also, some auto component industries seek advanced technologies, which force them to go to foreign partners, as those are not available in the country.

For both the automobile and the auto components industry, roads have a very important role in transportation as it carries about 65 per cent of freight and 85 per cent of passenger traffic.[3] Auto Policy of 2002 also mentions of low volume sale, fragmentation, inadequate R&D and technology support, lower productivity, limited resources for international market, and establishment of an efficient supply chain as the few challenges faced by the industry currently. Therefore, it mentions three major policy initiatives required to overcome these challenges:

The initiatives related to investments, tariffs and imports in line with the WTO commitments:

- Higher resource allocation to highways along with upgradation of those and improvement with infrastructure to accommodate increased number of vehicles; and
- The appropriate regulatory framework in tariff, environmental aspects and safety.

The Business Outlook Survey 2002-03 of 138 auto components manufacturers reveal that intense price competition in the international market has been the primary limiting factor in growth of exports as expected. They feel that quality is not a big concern for the growth of exports, but rather facing the competitive world price is the more pressing need.

---

3. *Source:* Government of India Auto Policy, 2002.

State-Level Policy and Implementation Initiatives

This section discusses the initiatives of the government of Maharashtra in taking advantage of the trade liberalisation policy for its domestic automotive industry.

Trends in Automotive Industry in Maharashtra and the Role of State Government

According to Mr. V.K. Jairath, Maharashtra's Principal Secretary for Industries, the primary reason for investors' interests in Maharashtra in the automobile and auto component industry is its higher productivity over other states. In a recent interview,[4] he notes that a factory in Maharashtra, in comparison with factories in any other states, employs 2 per cent extra labour, 16 per cent more capital because of higher land acquisition cost, with a 37 per cent more output and 51 per cent more value addition.

Among many other reasons, it is believed that the presence of about 30 to 40 per cent of ACMA (Automotive Components Manufacturers' Association) members in Maharashtra also contributes to the growth of this sector. The industrial areas built by Maharashtra Industrial Development Corporation (MIDC) at Pune, Talegaon, Chakan and the five-star industrial estate at Ranjangaon are well-connected by road. But as Maharashtra has recently started slipping behind states like Uttarakhand and Himachal Pradesh in attracting new investment to this sector,[5] the state government has launched the Mega Project Policy in 2005, offering customised packages for industries. It decided to provide the industries not only fiscal incentives, but incentives for fiscal infrastructure and manpower. From that point onwards, again the investment into the state has started to increase to an extent of 10,000 to 12,000 crore with the Mahindra-Logan project of Mahindra & Mahindra (M&M) in the year 2005, which rolled out its first car in April 2007.

To name a few major investments in this sector in Maharashtra: Volkswagen has plans to invest Rs. 2,450 crore with a manufacturing

4. Interview with the Principal Secretary, Industries, Maharashtra, Mr. V.K. Jairath, published in *Auto Monitor*, 8 June 2007. *Source: http://www.automonitor.co.in/article/Interview-with-Principal-Secretary,-Industries,-Maharashtra,-VK-Jairath/page1.html*, accessed on 1 June 2009.

5. Ibid.

capacity of 1.10 lakh units annually; DaimlerChrysler has already started the construction of its new plant of Mercedes Benz at Chakan in Pune that can manufacture 15,000 cars per year; and Mahindra Renault, a joint venture between the M&M and Renault of France has already launched its Logan from the M&M's plant at Nashik. It shows that Pune has developed as an automatic hub of India with its close forward and backward linkages in the state (Mitra, 2007). While Volkswagen decided to set up the plant, it was considering some other states like Andhra Pradesh, Tamil Nadu and Punjab, but finally zeroed in on the Chakan location due to its proximity to port, availability of skilled manpower and reliable logistics.

The auto component cluster in Pune consists of more than 500 SMEs, 20 per cent of whom are exporters. The SMEs serve to both the OEMs and the replacement market. The presence of the Pune-Mumbai knowledge corridor and the expansion of automobile industry in the Pune region have helped the auto component industry to grow as well.

Recently, land acquisition has become a major issue for most of the states and the manufacturing industries in particular. Maharashtra has not faced much of the same problems in this respect till a few years back. According to Mr. V.K. Jairath, MIDC has acquired and developed about 1,60,000 acres of land in Maharashtra during the last 40 years with its rather simple policy of paying the 'right' return on the foregone land. The state believes that by involving the farmers from the very beginning—offering them a piece in the development and offering jobs to the family members—would make acquisition easier. However, as not more than 30 per cent of total land available in Maharashtra is fit for irrigation, the farmers usually agree to accept the price for their rainfed lands. Now, MIDC has started to create land bank from the barren lands in Maharashtra, to develop those as five-star industrial estate, as has been done in Ranjangaon.

Concluding this section on the role of state in the development of automotive industry in Maharashtra, we can quote Oman (1999), which highlights a case study on the competition between the states of Tamil Nadu and Maharashtra to attract the investment of the Ford Foundation auto plant. It was a $400 million (about Rs. 1,868 crore) investment by this joint venture of Ford-Mahindra for the production of automobiles primarily for the domestic market. Ford Motors initially considered certain localities in Delhi, Bangalore, Tamil Nadu and Maharashtra, as the site for their plant. After initial screening, Ford chose Tamil Nadu over Maharashtra, even if the latter was home to its partner M&M, as well as several other automobile manufacturers.

Ford's primary reason for selecting Tamil Nadu, as described in its own survey, was that the company gave highest importance to the availability of skilled labour and a parts supplier base. Next in importance was the availability of infrastructure, particularly, proximity to sea port and container terminal over the proximity to airports, as they planned for large amount of exports and imports through trucks and ships. The next important factor was the incentives provided by the Tamil Nadu government, including a 14-year exemption from the state sales tax levied on the vehicles sold within the state, and the sales tax levied by the Central government on vehicles produced in the state but sold outside the state. The latter was to be paid by the state government on behalf of Ford-Mahindra. The company expected to sell 90 per cent of its outputs outside the state. Ford has specifically mentioned in the referred interview that the tax-relief incentives are most important among all incentives, since it results in a large amount of tax relief as the production keeps expanding.

Among other incentives provided by the Tamil Nadu government to Ford-Mahindra was provision of free-hold land by the state government, power-tariff concession for four years, some sort of water supply scheme, and an offer to build a sewage plant. The title of land seemed to be most important to the company among all these. The 'free-hold' ownership provided by the Tamil Nadu government, instead of a leased land was one of the major reasons for selecting this state over Maharashtra, as the latter did not agree on providing the 'free-hold' ownership. Another important factor was the labour problem that Mahindra had been facing in its Maharashtra location, and that drove away Ford from selecting Maharashtra for this new venture.

The last one to be mentioned here—making a difference between the states in investment decision by the Ford—was the combined effort of the government and industry associations in creating a business-friendly environment. It seemed that the parts suppliers in Tamil Nadu made a significant effort to present their case as a favourable location and the senior managers of these firms actively lobbied the state government in favour of Ford via industry associations. Therefore, this case study establishes the fact that infrastructure and connectivity are important, too, along with incentives for attracting investment in the state; and the state leaders or state-level industry associations can be expected to work as the active leader of the state for this purpose.

Initiatives in the State, Bureaucracy and Implementation

Just like in most manufacturing industries, growth in the automobile industry also depends on the availability of infrastructure, to a large extent. The following section will discuss Maharashtra's initiatives in building sufficient and reliable infrastructure. The initiatives in the power sector and ports having been earlier described; this section will focus on other areas relevant to the growth of automotive industry.

Even as Maharashtra has one of the country's best port facilities served by two major ports at JNPT (Jawaharlal Nehru Port Trust) and Mumbai, they seem to be insufficient amidst increasing demand of the port traffic. Maharashtra's contribution to the country's exports is 25 per cent. Since its ports serve the neighbouring states of Gujarat and Madhya Pradesh, about 40 per cent of exports of the country pass through these two ports, creating increasing amount of pressure on the port infrastructure. The average turnaround time at JNPT is 1.72 days, which is the lowest among all ports in the country; it is 5.6 days at Mumbai port. The average pre-berthing time is 1.39 days for JNPT and 1.37 days for Mumbai port, as compared to only 0.87 days for Cochin. The average idle time at berth is the lowest, that is 0.12 days at JNPT, whereas it is 1.11 days at Mumbai port.[6] The export dwell time for containerised sea freight at Mumbai port is three to five days, as compared to the international standard of less than 18 hours (Panagariya, 2008: 270). Therefore, along with expansion of capacity at JNPT, the state is also encouraging setting up of major six-seven ports along the 720 km long coastline of Maharashtra on a public-private partnership model.

---

6. MEDC (2002a). p.66, Table V.T.

Among the recent development of roads, the expansion of Mumbai-Nashik highway to four lanes is proceeding a bit slowly, but after its completion, there is a proposal to expand it to an expressway, like the one connecting Mumbai and Pune. The state departments are also toying with the idea of a dedicated freight corridor at railways.

Apart from infrastructure, the availability of skilled manpower is also an important factor in determining the pace of growth of the automobile and auto component industry. Without these components, productivity declines, the cost of production increases, and the manufacturing unit loses out in global competition. In this respect, Maharashtra is planning to create a labour market information cell, comprising representatives from educational institutions and the industries department. The cell will determine the skill requirements of the industries and provide trainings.

One primary factor helping spur growth in Maharashtra's automobile industry has been the establishment of the Automotive Research Association of India (ARAI) in 1966 near the industrial belt at Pune. The ARAI is responsible for providing technical expertise in R&D, testing, certification, homologation and framing of vehicle regulation, along with ensuring safe, less polluting and more efficient vehicle production.

Pune continued to grow as a major automotive hub with the setting up of the Auto Cluster Development and Research Institute Ltd. (ACDRIL) in the city in April 2004. It is an independent industry-driven company set up as a joint initiative of the Department of Industrial Policy and Promotion, Ministry of Commerce and Industry, Government of India; the Pimpri-Chinchwad Municipal Corporation (PCMC), Government of Maharashtra; and Maratha Chamber of Commerce, Industry and Agriculture (MCCIA). The institute was established under the Industrial Infrastructure Upgradation Scheme (IIUS), 2003 of the Government of India, with the primary purpose of improving the competitiveness of the Indian automotive industry in the global market through innovation, product design, R&D support, testing facilities, design centres, information hub, and assistance with appropriate technology transfer. All the auto component manufacturers, including the rubber and polymer associations, renowned institutions including engineering colleges, R&D institutions, banks, financial institutions and various government agencies, are involved in this project. This helps the Pune region to grow as a major automotive hub in the country. At present, the city is home to large players like, Bajaj Auto, Bajaj Tempo, DaimlerChrysler, Fiat India, Kinetic Engineering and Piaggio Vehicles, with the last one located at Baramati in Pune district. The Pune auto cluster, which is the first of its kind in the state, commenced operations in January 2006.

In August 2006, General Motors (GM) inked a deal with the government of Maharashtra to invest about $300 million (about Rs. 1,400 crore) to set up a Greenfield plant in Talegaon, near Pune. This facility is supposed to have a production capacity of 1.40 lakh cars per year, capable of creating 1,000 jobs. This facility is supposed to double GM's already existing facility of small cars in Halol, near Vadodara, Gujarat. About 300 acres of land has been leased out by MIDC for 95 years. This expands the scope of exports of component suppliers in this area as GM decided to move its suppliers' base from other countries to India.

The Pune city also has a substantial presence of auto component manufacturers and the state's automotive industry has a good amount of backward and forward integration. It has support from the country's major auto components suppliers, along with the advantage of being close to the country's financial capital to supply the additional services like finance and insurance. There are several institutional supports in the Pune cluster in the form of technical aspects, education, management, research institutions and associations.

MIDC has developed several five-star industrial areas with special infrastructure facilities. The primary objective of the five-star industrial areas developed by MIDC was to attract foreign investment. There are four such five-star industrial areas that facilitate the growth of the automobile and auto component industry by attracting a good amount of foreign investment. Among them, the MIDC industrial park at Ranjangaon has certain location advantages. It is located 50 km away from the Pune-Ahmednagar highway and is a one-hour drive to the Pune airport. It is also well-connected to Aurangabad via Ahmednagar. This Ranjangaon industrial area is categorised either 'B' or 'C' from the aspects of providing incentives by the government. There are also several auto component manufacturers, e.g., manufacturers of tyres, steel products, in this industrial area.

Another five-star industrial park in Maharashtra that contributed to the development of automotive industry is Sinnar, just 30 km away from Nashik and 185 km from Pune. This place is well-connected by railway and road to Mumbai; and another expressway has been conceived between the cities of Mumbai, Pune and Nashik, to create a Golden Triangle. MIDC has also taken care of the power supply and water supply issues. MIDC and Maharashtra State Electricity Board (MSEB) have set up a 132-KV substation. Sinnar industrial area is categorised as 'C' or 'D' for the purpose of industrial incentives.

The third such five-star industrial park of MIDC at Shendre is just 8 km away from Aurangabad airport and 19 km away from the railway station. MIDC has arranged for uninterrupted power supply and ample water supply sourcing from the river Godavari after purification is conducted according to World Health Organization standards. The 66 metre wide main road and 25 to 30 metre wide internal roads are parts of this industrial park. This is a 'C' category for purposes of industrial incentives.

The fourth such five-star industrial park at Butibori is 20 km away from the Nagpur airport on the NH-7 connected to Hyderabad. Nagpur railway station is only 28 km away from the industrial park. Nagpur itself has a strong industrial presence, with a 'cargo hub' in the implementation stage to work as a dry port. Among the major auto makers, M&M is making the world's largest tractor plant at Butibori, and Ashok Leyland has its second plant at Bhandara which is about 70 km from Nagpur. This is 'D' category for purposes of incentives.

Apart from the five-star industrial areas, there are more than 75 other industrial areas from Thane district supporting different sectors and some of them have developed as an automotive hub of Maharashtra.

The MIDC industrial park at Chakan is on the Talegaon-Ahmednagar highway, which is 30 km from Pune. There is reliable road connectivity through Mumbai-Pune expressway and travel time to Mumbai is approximately three hours. There are also several auto components manufacturing companies in this cluster, such as Minda Industries, Kalyani Lemmerz, Keihin Tai, Atlas Copco and some vendors of Bajaj Auto. The latter has set up a very large unit in this area, too. This 'C' category industrial area receives a good amount of incentives from the government of Maharashtra. Volkswagen, the world's fourth largest car maker has set up its biggest manufacturing plant expanding to about 500 acres of land, with an investment of about US$ 300 million (that is, Rs. 1,400 crore). It has decided to launch a small car by the second quarter of 2009; the project is supposed to create 2,500 jobs. The state industrial policy must have worked as a boost for FDI in this sector as Volkswagen has become the third European automobile company within a month after Daimler-Chrysler and Renault, to sign a memorandum of understanding with the government of Maharashtra for setting up the plants.

Another such major automobile hub in Maharashtra is Nashik, which houses India's largest multi-utility vehicle manufacturer, M&M. It is also the country's largest tractor manufacturer, which is assembled in its Kandivali, Mumbai plant. Nashik is also a home to several large component manufacturers, such as Anand group's Piston plant and ancillary units of M&M.

The last emerging auto hub in the state to be mentioned is at Aurangabad. Back in the year 2005, Maharashtra government had set up a special purpose vehicle to set up the Aurangabad Automobile Industrial Cluster (AAIC) costing about Rs. 31.45 crore at Waluj. This facility was the second such auto cluster after that in Pune. This cluster has facilities like raw material testing and inspection laboratory, costing about Rs. 9 crore. The proposed R&D centre for product innovation—with tool room and CAD/CAM facilities—was to be created at the cost of Rs. 14.26 crore. The above R&D facility has been supported by a marketing and export promotion cell, a waste management plant, warehouses for aluminium and steel, and logistics and packaging units. Although Bajaj had its plant set up at Waluj in the late 1980s, the place is still a 'D' class as categorised for purposes of determining incentives. This area is developing fast as another major automobile hub due to the recent interest of foreign auto companies, like Skoda India, for its Octavia project at Shendre site. The role of the state government in developing this cluster is definitely important as it is a part of the Maharashtra government's initiative to develop the Marathwada region with a corpus of Rs. 3,307 crore.

Recent Performance of the State and Issues for the State Government

If the Indian auto industry hopes to make its mark in the world map, one major area to be addressed is about making it cost-efficient in order for it to have a place in the global competition. The inter-state anomalies in tax policies, incentives and emission norms, should be minimised in order to smooth out the movements of goods and relocation of industries and that the geographical spread of this industry does not affect the supply chain (NCAER, 2003; Narayanan and Vashisht, 2008; WTC, 2008).

For example, at present, Maharashtra is the only state to be still continuing with octroi tax, whereas some other states are also continuing with distortionary subsidies. Octroi has been one major source of revenue collection by states, which act as a major impediment to inter-state trade, as it is collected during entry of goods in any local area for consumption and sales. After liberalisation till date, this has been one of the most discussed sources of taxes in the state and various committees have already recommended for the complete abolition of this tax for the free float in inter-state trade. The municipal government in Maharashtra, however, has found it difficult to abolish the system of octroi. The primary reason is that they have been unable to design an alternative source for the same amount of tax revenue. In the recent few years, this has been slowly abolished from most of the states, except for Maharashtra. A few years ago, the states of Uttar Pradesh, Gujarat and Rajasthan, replaced octroi with surcharge on sales tax; meanwhile, the states of Karnataka and Madhya Pradesh replaced it with entry tax.

Octroi not only affects the inter-state trade of Maharashtra, but also makes the products from this state less competitive in the outside world. This way of revenue collection creates an adverse impact on economic efficiency and resource allocation. Although the present chief minister of Maharashtra has promised that all octroi will be abolished by the middle of 2008, that goal is still far away. Moreover, since the rate of octroi is determined and collected by the respective municipal bodies, its rate is quite varied even across municipal areas. It creates inefficiency in distribution of industries, as people tend to develop industries where they get raw materials cheaper (see Rao and Rao, 2005-06). As mentioned by some executives of MEDC in a seminar[7] that Bajaj Auto has recently shifted their location out of Akrudi due to the octroi level in the state, and the state government needs to take care of this trade-distorting tax soon.

If the financial incentives provided to the industry across states would have fewer anomalies, then a competitive environment would bring out the most suitable places to develop the industry. Recently, states like Maharashtra, Gujarat, Uttarakhand and West Bengal[8] started competing with each other with matching incentives to attract automobile industries. But when the matching incentives are offered by several states together, it puts them on the same platform, wasting the state resources spent on incentives, which could instead be used for developmental purposes. The hosts of taxes and incentives increase the discretionary power of bureaucracy, too. The investment decision in any state should not be based on the incentives or subsidies offered, rather that should be based on the real factors such as infrastructure, availability of skills, and political climate, to do business and sustainability.

One of the largest and oldest automobile industries in the state of Maharashtra is Tata Motors. It started the first plant in the eastern part of the country at Jamshedpur, then continued to scatter at different places, such as Pune, Lucknow and then to Pantnagar in Uttarakhand and Dharwad in Karnataka. Two primary reasons for the industry's decision to diffuse its presence are the following: so that they will not invest all of their resources in one location; and to reduce the risk of investment. In this way, they can minimise the risk amidst any geographical, natural or political turmoil. Before taking a decision about putting in their investment in a location, industry looks for a few things, including the following: that the plant be close to the market; it be accessible by a port and with good connectivity; and that the investment be provided adequate support from the state government.[9] Their initial plant in Chinchwad, near Pune, was

7. Seminar attended by me on *Export Competitiveness of Maharashtra*, held on August 12, 2008 at World Trade Centre, a joint collaboration between WTC and MEDC.

8. The period of discussion limits us to the fact when the government of West Bengal also tried to attract Tata Motors through several incentives, to set up a plant at Singur. Later, in the year 2008, when the plan did not work out in West Bengal, the government of Gujarat attracted that investment, whereas, it is heard that government of Maharashtra was among the competitors too.

9. Interview with one senior executive of Tata Motors in Mumbai, 5 May and 8 August 2008, Mumbai.

set up at a time when the area was not yet developed; hence they received the incentives under a specific scheme. After several years of production, the area developed fast, improving the standard of living and cost of living, which made the state government to announce it as an "A" category area for the purpose of determining incentives. This stopped the company from being eligible to receiving incentives from the state government, which discouraged the company and motivated them to expand its production in other states offering what for them were better incentives.

Even with policies based on incentives through concession in indirect taxes (done primarily for exports), usually the state governments are supposed to reimburse the tax amount to the business house after it is paid. This creates a complicated system, and most of the time, it becomes a liability of the company to collect the reimbursement from the state government. Thus, this kind of incentive-based policies may help the state in attracting investments at the beginning, but it is not sustainable unless backed by developmental initiatives, such as development of port facilities, power, roads and transport facilities.

Power shortage in Maharashtra having been a major problem in the last few years, this industry is also getting affected. The large OEMs can reduce their production temporarily, or shift their production to their other plants in other locations across the country, but the small components manufacturers usually need to shut the production. In a recent regulation, if the power shortage exceeds 4500 MW in any industry, they need to cut down the work week from six days a week to five days. Hence, industries may not be able to meet increasing demand if the situation is not addressed immediately. The power shortage has created problems in production of two major automobile companies of the state, namely, Tata Motors and M&M.

Maharashtra has the advantage of having one of the most automated, advanced and efficient ports like JNPT with two dedicated terminals; one container terminal to handle container vessels, and one bulk terminal for dry cargo for vessels of up to 70,000 DWT. Out of its total capacity of 13.5 million tonnes, 7.5 million tonnes, 3.5 million tonnes, and 2.5 million tonnes are shared between the container, dry bulk and liquid bulk terminals, respectively. Recently, the ports have been facing various problems, primarily from the inability to manage the increasing amount of port traffic. One of the major problems for the automotive industry about the port is that the vehicle parking facilities in the ports are not very good. Vehicles sometimes need to wait for a few days in the port before getting a clearance for exports. If the facility is not good, the produce get damaged and become unacceptable for exports. If there are good vehicle maintenance facility at ports, then the vehicles can be immediately taken care of its damages without bringing it back again to the city before the final export.[10] Another problem at port is the time taken for loading and unloading, which sometimes takes three or four days as compared to three to four hours in other countries. The main reason for this delay is that the waiting time for the vessels to reach for loading is much higher in India, which needs to be addressed to improve the competitiveness of exports. One primary reason for this delay in the port is the port traffic. Since Maharashtra ports are handling a major portion of India's international trade, the port facility needs to be expanded to accommodate the increasing amount of traffic.

Finally, the state-level anomalies in labour laws need to be repaired along with flexibilities in labour laws. Labour being in the concurrent list, the implementation issue of any law related to this lies on the state. In this respect, Panagariya (2008) suggests that the state government can provide the SEZ a public utility status, which prevents the conduct of workers' strikes in factories without prior notice. Also, as suggested by one senior executive of Tata Motors,[11] all non-core activities in the automobile sector should be permitted to use contract labour, whereas the core activities could be done by the permanent labour. The labour standards need to be uniform for any skill-based industries. This can also be done through state initiatives by creating a pool of skilled labour as required by the industry.

Concluding Note

Maharashtra has been a major hub for the automobile and auto components industry for the last few decades. The government's initiatives initially have proven to be successful in attracting investment for this industry. The backward and forward linkages through the availability of

10. Ibid.

11. Ibid.

skilled labour, supply of automobile components and infrastructure support—such as power and port facilities—along with increasing amount of domestic and international demand, helped the industry in its drive for expansion after economic liberalisation.

Recently, however, Maharashtra has lost some big projects from automobile companies to other states like Uttarakhand and Himachal Pradesh, both of which are growing to become good competitors in the industry. Since these two states receive central funds, states like Maharashtra perhaps finds it difficult to match that aid coming from the Central government with their own incentive schemes. Moreover, incentive-based schemes for attracting investment do not seem to be sustainable in the long term. Hence, it needs to use its own advantages, through the expansion of port facilities, captive power generation for uninterrupted power supply, by strengthening the existing auto component industry to maintain the backward linkage, and using the 'financial capital of India' in generating domestic demand. It would serve Maharashtra well if it focuses on these strengths instead of competing through unsustainable modes, such as incentives.

The current system of three tiers of emission norms in the state can perhaps also be resolved in order to facilitate reduction of cost for the industry. There seems to be two immediate issues that the state can take care of in order to encourage industry and investment in the state, and these are more important for the manufacturing industry and more encouraging for the state exporting units of goods. The first one is the assurance of faster movement of goods from the plant to their destinations, particularly for the exports; and the second one is faster processing of reimbursement of indirect taxes for the eligible exports. These are possible under the state SEZ units; hence, the onus to improve international trade through these avenues lies on the state machinery. Finally, labour laws can be made flexible, in turn reducing the scope of industrial disputes, and state initiatives can be extended to meet the industrial demand of skilled workforce as well.

CASE STUDY II: PHARMACEUTICAL INDUSTRY

Introduction: Growth of Indian Pharmaceutical Industry, Internal and External Trade

The Indian pharmaceutical industry is worth US$8.8 billion industry and the market is the fourth largest in the world, holding a significant position in the world market in terms of volume. According to the recent IMS Health report, the global pharmaceutical sale in 2006-07 was US$643 billion, with US in the top position, followed by Europe. The share of Indian pharmaceutical industry in the global market is increasing at a rate of 10 per cent per year on average. The pharmaceutical industry in India ranks fourth in terms of volume and 13th in terms of sales all over the world. Moreover, it contributes a huge 20-24 per cent of the world's generic drugs.[12]

The output of this sector grew more than ten-fold from Rs. 5,000 crore in 1990 to over Rs. 55,000 crore in 2005-06. The exports grew as well, reaching to more than 200 countries around the world including highly regulated markets of developed countries, like the US, Europe, Japan and Australia. In 1999-2000, the exports of drugs and pharmaceutical industry were Rs. 6,631 crore out of a total production of Rs. 19,737 crore. The exports grew from Rs. 7,857.80 crore in 2004-05 to over Rs. 21,000 crore in 2005-06.[13] An increasing number of Indian pharmaceutical companies are getting approvals from agencies like US FDA (US Food and Drug Administration) and some other countries, such as UK, Australia and South Africa. India has the largest number of US FDA approved manufacturing facilities outside the US.

The major contribution of Indian pharmaceutical sector in the world market started with the product patent regime for food, chemical and pharmaceutical products under the Patent (Amendment) Act, April 2005 to meet India's commitments under trade-related aspects of intellectual property rights (TRIPs) of WTO. For the last 20 years before this product

12. *Source:* WTC Research Study on Export Competitiveness of Maharashtra, 2008.

13. *Source:* Business Portal of India: Industry and Services, a Government of India e-governance initiative, *http://business.gov.in*, accessed on 5 June 2009.

patent regime, the patents were only granted for the process. Indian pharmaceutical companies have been taking advantage of this process patent regime, holding a major share of the world's generic market. But after the opening of the economy beginning in 1991, multinational pharmaceutical companies have also become interested in the Indian market and domestic companies are engaging in international trade of their pharmaceutical generic products. The introduction of product patent regime has encouraged Indian pharmaceutical companies to invest in R&D activities to establish themselves in the global discovery-led platform. At present, out of about 24,000 pharmaceutical SMEs in the country, more than 1,200 are engaged in exports; they, however, lack knowledge of IPR to expand and sustain their business in the pharmaceutical export market under the WTO regime. The Indian government's initiatives—such as the introduction of amendments to the Patent Act of 1970, R&D efforts, and some more policy initiatives to be discussed in the next section—are expected to bring in the benefits of TRIPs in the near future in terms of international trade figures.

The next few sections are arranged as follows:

- Section II discusses the union trade policy and the policies of the Government of India that are important for international trade activities in the pharmaceutical sector.
- Section III deals with trade-related policies for this sector in Maharashtra. The two parts of this section constitute policy changes at the state level, state-level institutions; and the initiatives of Maharashtra in policy implementations.
- Section IV summarises the performance of this particular industry in the state.
- Section V concludes the case study.

Union Trade Policy and Related Policies for this Sector

The basic objectives of the Government of India regarding the drug and pharmaceutical sector have been drafted in the Drug Policy of 1986. While those objectives remain largely valid even today, there have been a number of necessary modifications and some additions of policies that were required to face the global competition after liberalisation and the WTO agreement. Hence, the Drug Policy of 1986 was modified in 1994. The process of liberalisation in 1991 began the process of removing industrial licensing for the manufacture of all drugs and pharmaceutical products, except for few bulk drugs produced using some specific technologies. In the year 1999, government again opened up those five specific drugs for private sector production, which were earlier reserved only for the public sector. Foreign investment through automatic route has been raised from 51 per cent to 74 per cent in 2000 and then to 100 per cent. The automatic approval of foreign technology agreement in case of all bulk drugs, their intermediates and formulations, except for the few produced by the use of recombinant technology, led the growth of India's contract research and manufacturing industry. The public sector units that are into the production of drugs and pharmaceuticals have been opened to face competition from imports and have been privatised, wherever possible.

There was a huge reduction of non-tariff barriers to imports as mentioned in the EXIM policies. Drugs and Cosmetics Act and Rules introduced a centralised system of registration. The Ministry of Health and Family Welfare is supposed to enforce a strict regulatory process for the import of bulk drugs and formulations.

For encouraging the pharmaceutical companies in research and development, Pharmaceutical Research and Development Committee (PRDC) was set up in the year 1999, under the chairmanship of the Director General of Council of Scientific and Industrial Research (CSIR). This committee suggested some local standards for qualifying as an R&D unit in India. These include the following criteria for the R&D unit:

- Invest at least 5 per cent of its turnover per annum in R&D;
- Invest at least Rs. 10 crore per annum in innovative research;
- Employ at least 100 research scientists in R&D in India;
- Have been granted at least 10 patents for research done in India; and,
- Own and operate manufacturing facilities in India.

The introduction in Parliament of the Patent (Second Amendment) Bill—granting extension of patent life to 20 years—has been one major step to meet the commitment of liberalisation under WTO. India's policy initiatives in this sector has given it the recognition of being a low-cost producer and it has become one of the world's major suppliers of bulk drugs during the last one and a half decades after liberalisation. However, in the attempt to implement the country's obligations under TRIPs, allowing both process and product patent, India needed to address the impact of that on the long-term competitiveness of Indian industry. Hence, the Pharmaceutical Policy 2002 was formulated with a reorientation of its earlier objectives. The importance of improving incentives to encourage research and development in this sector to sustain in the competition after the patent law, and the need to reduce further price control in view of liberalisation, were two primary concerns of government in the policy that was laid down in 2002.

Some recent policy measures in the last few budgets also have roles to play in the changing dynamics of this sector. The 2004-05 Budget has mandated that all drugs and materials used for clinical trials be exempted from customs and excise duty. This has actually encouraged some of the pharmaceutical or biotechnology companies to extend their operations to clinical trials.

The 2005-06 Budget plans to increase the corpus for R&D funds phase-wise, along with stable policy environments and incentives to help the Indian biotechnology and pharmaceutical industries in their drive to be recognised in the world market. The reduction of corporate tax from 35 to 30 per cent and reduction of customs duty for nine specified pharmaceutical and biotechnology machineries in the budget of 2005-06, will encourage both industries to engage in R&D activities.

The setting up of the National Institute of Pharmaceutical Education and Research (NIPER) by the Government of India is a move towards achieving excellence in pharmaceutical sciences, technologies, education and training. The institute is supposed to work on collaborative research with the industry and other technical institutes in the area of drug discovery and pharmaceutical technology development.

Trade-Related Policies of Maharashtra

State-level Institutions and Policy Changes, Bureaucracy

The Maharashtra government has expressed its intentions and commitments towards the growth of the biotechnology industry through financial incentives, infrastructure support and some other specific benefits with the formulation of the Biotechnology Policy of 2001. This policy also boosts the development of the pharmaceutical industry in the state as these two industries are closely associated. The financial incentives include empowering a separate committee at the national level for the decision on sales tax and VAT, capital subsidy for small-scale biotechnology (BT) units, providing incentives as eligible under 'D' category area under package scheme of incentives, and refund of octroi and similar levies. Among the infrastructure facilities, the BT units enjoy industrial/agricultural power tariffs, get exemption from statutory power cuts and from electricity duty, get lands at concessional rates for centre of excellence in the BT unit. Captive power generation is permitted in BT units. It gets twice admissible FSI (floor space index) for BT units in the park and they get incentives applicable to the IT units. One of the primary objectives of the Biotechnology Policy of 2001 is to help the state develop cost-effective affordable drugs and devices to counter common diseases of tropical and sub-tropical areas. The policy document also mentions the requirement of simplifying the application of labour laws and procedures to expedite the growth of the biotechnology sector.

In the Industrial Policy of 2001, the state has shown its willingness to amend certain provisions of the Industrial Disputes Act and the Contract Labour Act, provided it gets the approval of the Central government and the legislature. The state has decided to share its large storage of data on public health with the biotechnology companies through what it calls a 'transparent and ethical manner'. The public health machinery of the state should actively collaborate with biotechnology companies in clinical research following international norms. For an efficient plan towards treatment of urban wastes and industrial effluents, state municipal bodies and organisations such as CIDCO, MHADA, Maharashtra Jeevan Pradhikaran (MJP) and MIDC, have been provided the responsibilities of taking up the projects with biotechnology companies. It has been decided that the existing infrastructure and the data should be made available to the biotechnology companies for experimentation in this project.

Maharashtra's Food and Drug Administration (FDA) is the state's primary regulatory body for the protection of consumers. The commissioner is the administrative head of the administration and drug control laboratory. Its headquarter is in Mumbai, with offices in divisions and district places. Its authority covers the following:

- Issuance of certificates under the WHO Good Manufacturing Practices scheme;
- Analysing sample drugs at Drug Control laboratory in Mumbai and Aurangabad; and,
- Information dissemination through meetings, lectures and organisation of seminars.

The Maharashtra Food and Drug Administration has been given the responsibility to play an active role in facilitating the growth and development of the country's pharmaceutical industry. In 1970, the circle offices were created in places like Akola, Kolhapur and Nashik, and the assistant commissioner at circle offices were declared as the licensing authorities to grant selling licences for the respective circles. In 1975, after some expansion, the post of assistant commissioner and joint commissioner were created at the divisional places and district places, respectively. Till 1990, the joint commissioner (headquarters) remained as the licensing authority for granting manufacturing licences for the entire state, and the joint commissioners/assistant commissioners were given the power for the grant of selling licences in their respective areas. But from 1990, the divisional joint commissioner was given the authority to grant licence for drug manufacturing in their respective divisions, making Maharashtra the forerunner in decentralising the licensing process for manufacturing to the divisional level. This decentralisation definitely helped to reduce the amount of bureaucratic delay for setting up new manufacturing plants in the state.

The state government has also decided to encourage the setting up of 'centres of excellence' for research and development in life sciences and technology, where such centres will be approved on an individual basis and will be provided land at concessional rates. In the same Biotechnology Policy of 2001, the state government also made a committment to help set up biotechnology parks, research and development centres and pilot plant facilities for contract research, through its equity stakes in kind, such as by allotting land for the projects. The state government's commitment to create a biotechnology resource centre for certification of products after testing, and an experimental animal facility meeting the ethical standards, signifies the state's willingness to attract the biotechnology and pharmaceutical industry. Moreover, in recent times—given how land acquisition is the biggest problem for any industry in most states—the state government's commitment to provide land to the biotech and bio-pharma industries has created a positive impact on prospective investors.

Finally, the state government has realised that the pharmaceutical industry requiring large amount of investments, and India being a signatory of WTO, the development of this industry can only be encouraged through provision of intellectual property protection. Since the state cannot make policies regarding IPR, the government has decided to provide a special manpower-training programme through the University of Pune in creating awareness about intellectual property protection. The university is already having its first CSIR chair in IPR.

The state has some of the country's premier research institutes that help supply skilled manpower to the industry; with such a strong knowledge base, it becomes even more attractive to multinationals. Among these are the National Chemical Laboratory (NCL) at Pune; University Department of Chemical Technology (UDCT); Bhabha Atomic Research Centre (BARC); Tata Institute of Fundamental Research (TIFR); Indian Institute of Technology (IIT) and Cancer Research Institute (CRI). Recognising that the development of any knowledge-based industry depends heavily on the availability of skilled manpower, the state government has emphasised in its Biotechnology Policy of 2001 that the pharma biotech park be developed in Pune.

The Ministry of Commerce & Industry set up the Pharmaceuticals Export Promotion Council (PHARMEXCIL) in 2004 with recommendations from four major pharmaceutical associations, for the promotion of exports. It has its regional offices in Delhi, Mumbai and Chennai, which provide all export-related information along with export promotion activities. The Mumbai office is working actively for the cause and the government of Maharashtra needs to take their opinion into consideration for the growth of the industry in the state.

Recently, the Indian government made plans to open the country's first pharmaceutical patent filing facilitation centre in Hyderabad, followed by two more cities, Delhi and Mumbai. The Ministry of Chemicals and Fertilizers, which oversees the pharmaceutical sector, has allocated Rs. 1 crore for this project. These centres will help the pharmaceutical companies, particularly, the small and the medium-size ones, to file patents within and outside the country. This facilitation centre is being set up by the PHARMEXCIL. The centre will encourage new discoveries, through patent filing, which can help the industries to learn how to capitalise the new patent regime and generate revenue from it.

In 2001, the state government noticed that several pharmaceutical units were moving outside the state from Thane, Mulund etc., particularly to places like Goa. The state government then announced some 'special package' to prevent this and to promote the development of the industry in Vidarbha, Marathwada regions.

The Industrial, Investment & Infrastructure Policy of Maharashtra, 2006 has identified strategies to serve its policy objectives. Among them, the important ones for growth of pharmaceutical industry are the following:

- Identification of thrust sectors;
- Building up of quality infrastructure;
- Attracting mega investment, both domestic and foreign;
- Strengthening the SME sector through promotion of quality competitiveness;
- Research & development and technology upgradation;
- Nurturing industrial clusters; and
- Smooth exit option for industries.

The thrust areas identified by the state government as priority are: infrastructure; some manufacturing industries including pharmaceutical sector; some services including IT and IT-enabled services; biotechnology, and establishment of gas distribution networks in major industrial areas in the state to supply cost-effective fuel.

The state initiative in development of industrial clusters should help the pharmaceutical industries through creation of industry linkages as it happened in the case of auto clusters in Maharashtra. These clusters can serve the specific needs of the industry. Smooth exit option is another important factor, particularly for industries involving high-risk investments depending on the success of high-skilled research and development, and pharmaceutical industry is one such. Thus, the state move seems to be in the right direction for the development of this industry, although it is too early to comment about the impact of this policy on the industry.

Initiatives in the State and Implementation

The Ministry of Small Scale Industry (SSI) of Government of India has taken initiatives to help develop SSIs across the country through a 'cluster development approach'. In July 2003, it selected 21 such clusters across the country, keeping in mind the following considerations: distinct technology and product; status of basic infrastructure; presence of capable supporting institutions; potential of growth; local leadership and support within clusters; and contribution to employment and exports.[14] Thane-Belapur belt in Maharashtra has been selected as one such cluster for manufacturing of bulk drugs in a part of the MIDC area, which is also known as Trans Thane Creek (TTC). It is understood that the initiative of Maharashtra government to decongest Mumbai, proximity to ports like JNPT and Bombay port trust, initiatives of CIDCO to develop Thane area and the presence of Thane Creek to facilitate disposal of industrial wastes, might be the primary reasons of selection of this area.

The other such concentration of basic and bulk drug units has been in Mumbai, Pune, Raigad and Tarapur belt. With the Biotech Park at Hinjawadi, Pune, a joint venture with The Chatterjee Group (TCG), the importance is given to the pharmaceutical biotechnology industry in Maharashtra. A patch of land measuring 136 acres has been taken for the development of phase II of the park, which is adjacent to the IT park. The nearby research institutions like Serum Institute of Pune, University of Pune and their skilled manpower are to support this park.

The BT-Gallup survey has placed Pune in the 5th rank for doing business among all Indian cities. It is close to the commercial capital of the country, Mumbai where a large number of the pharmaceutical industries are located and connected well through one of India's best highways, the Mumbai-Pune expressway. The core shared facility and the medico-clinical

14. *Source: http://www.smallindustryindia.com/publications/books/clusdev/ch5.pdf,* accessed on 5 June 2009.

facility housing research centre, bio-informatics lab, genomics and proteomics lab, the chemistry and bio-discovery labs, pre-clinical, clinical labs and analytics labs set up in the park in this joint venture with TCG, help other pharmaceutical industries in their supply chain. Moreover, the park houses a business facilitation centre, residential complex, service apartments and built to suit units. Infrastructure facilities provided at the park are roads (inland and waterways), ports and power supply. Among the infrastructure facilities, about six of the common effluent treatment plants (CETP) are under construction, and another six are in the planning stage. Eight sewage treatment plants (STP) are in the planning stage.

According to MIDC, the target industries for this park are the pharmaceutical and BT companies, clinical trial labs, contract research organisations, bio-informatics centres, vaccine production units, analytical labs and medical centres. Among the already existing units, Emcure and Shreya biotech has already started production with respective areas of 14 acres and 10 acres of land. USV has taken 10 acres of land and there are other large-scale Indian companies who are interested and their plans are being finalised. There are some international tie-ups, along with some research institutions and universities, international BT parks and knowledge parks. Development of the biotech park in Jalna also helps the pharmaceutical industry in the state. Overall, out of a total 21 SEZs notified in the state after the enforcement of the SEZ Act on October 2007, there are three pharmaceutical SEZs; one of them in Pune developed by Serum Bio Pharma, one developed by MIDC in Nanded, and the last one in Shendre five-star industrial area developed by Wockhardt Infrastructure Development Ltd. This establishes a strong presence of pharmaceutical industry in the state.

The presence of backward linkages—including availability of quality active ingredients from Gujarat, Rajasthan, Madhya Pradesh; solvents from various parts of Maharashtra and Gujarat; catalyst from local market; machineries for the bulk drug manufacturing in the Mumbai market; along with supply of skilled manpower—helped the industry to grow in these regions. A recent MEDC report[15] point to the fact that from the period August 1991 to January 2008, there were 442 projects approved in the

15. MEDC (2008). August.

pharmaceutical sector, representing about 3 per cent of the total number of projects approved in all the sectors in Maharashtra. The same report also mentions that the drugs and pharmaceutical sector brought about the number of 121 FDIs worth Rs. 1,012 crore during the period August 1991 to November 2007 in Maharashtra. This is about 3 per cent of total FDI of all sectors in the state.

Performance of the Industry in Maharashtra in Light of Liberalised Trade Policy

Maharashtra's initiative to develop its pharmaceutical industry is not as old as that of pioneer states like Andhra Pradesh and Karnataka. The developments in the last one decade, however, are indicative of a bright future for this industry of the state. In 2001, when Maharashtra formulated its first biotechnology policy, several major multinational and Indian corporations were already operating in those states.

According to a World Trade Centre Study on *Export Competitiveness of Maharashtra* (2008), there are about 10,000 manufacturing units, including 290 large-scale sectors and 45 multinational companies with manufacturing bases in India. The same study points out that Maharashtra contributes 40 per cent of the total turnover and 11 per cent of the total value of formulations to the pharmaceutical industry. The pharmaceutical exports from Maharashtra have been increasing consistently over the years. The above study finds that the export figure was about Rs. 106 billion in 2002-03, increasing to Rs. 250 billion in 2006-07, the latter being about 10 per cent of the country's total pharmaceutical exports.

Out of about 20,000 pharmaceutical manufacturers in India, 4,100 are registered in Maharashtra[16], with Mumbai-Thane being the major belt in the state. The other locations are Aurangabad, Nashik, Pune and Raigad districts. Some of the globally renowned companies are Pfizer, Glaxo Wellcome, Novartis, Johnson & Johnson, Abbott, Hoechst, Nicholas Piramal, Cipla, Lupin, Wockhardt, Rhone-Poulenc and Glenmark. Among them, Wockhardt has entered into a bio-pharmaceutical project with an

16. "Maharashtra's Economic Performance and Investment Climate", talking points by Chief Minister of Maharashtra, Mr. Vilasrao Deshmukh, at the CEO Roundtable, Maharashtra Investment Forum, New York, June 2007.

investment of about 125 crore. It has been allotted 100 acres of land for the purpose. Lupin and Nicholas Piramal are encouraging innovative drug research in a big way. According to the State Drug Control Authorities, there are about 130 pharmaceutical companies having the WHO GMP certification. This number is about 15 per cent of the total units certified in all over India under this scheme.

As is well-known, the country's pharmaceutical industry is primarily divided into generics and contract research manufacturing segments. Whereas not much is done in the discovery front, the two major hubs housing this industry are Thane of the Navi Mumbai area and Hinjawadi of Pune area. The former is primarily used by the generic companies and for basic drugs; the latter is occupied mainly by the contract research manufacturing companies such as Chembiotek of TCG and Emcure.

The Maharashtra FDA took initiatives to follow the amended GMP (good manufacturing practices) rules enacted by the Central government that came into force in the year 2005. Following that, 50 manufacturing licences were suspended due to non-compliance with guidelines provided for in Schedule M. About 400 units were found to be compliant. But the overall status of GMP compliance needs to improve. Manufacturing and sale of spurious drugs in the state is another growing concern. The shortage of FDA inspectors deputised in the state contributes to the problem. Although FDA in the state cannot recruit those inspectors, it should take the case forward to the Maharashtra Public Service Commission for recruitment.

According to Glenn Saldhana, Chief Executive Officer and Managing Director of Maharashtra-based Glenmark Pharmaceuticals, the factors that have helped the state become one of the country's pharmaceutical hubs include good infrastructure, better supply of raw materials, active pharmaceutical supplies and a huge pool of talent.[17]

Concluding Note

The Indian pharmaceutical industry has always been market-driven. The high volume and low priced market has been the driving force towards constant utilisation of superior technologies and maximised resource

17. See Mathew (2008).

allocation to maintain low production cost. During the last few years, Indian pharmaceutical industries moved up to a worth of more than two billion US dollars of M&A activities across the globe. There were about 62 global acquisitions by Indian pharmaceutical companies since the year 2000, which contributes to 20 per cent of all global M&As by Indian companies. Some of the major pharmaceutical companies, such as Dr. Reddy's, Wockhardt, Ranbaxy, Sun Pharmaceuticals and Nicholas Piramal, have done more than four such transactions and therefore acquired a larger market size in many of the European and American markets. These M&A have helped Indian pharmaceutical companies to function in foreign markets with their own manufacturing facilities, thus helping them to meet the local regulatory environments like control substances and government tenders. Besides the M&A activities, outsourcing by the major multinationals is also an option these days, where non-core activities of research and manufacturing process is done by the Indian companies.

Given the already existing pharmaceutical base of the country, Maharashtra has the potential to expand its share in the country's production as well as exports all over the world. The biggest problems faced by this industry in the state of Maharashtra currently are octroi, infrastructure bottlenecks and competition from other states through special offers of incentives, excise free zones and income tax holidays, all of which are driving away industries to the states of Himachal Pradesh, Uttarakhand and Jammu and Kashmir. The state needs to be more proactive to discuss issues with the PHARMEXICIL and develop an approach road to increase its share in global sales.

The World Bank's 2004 *Investment Climate Assessment* found that firms benefit most from their investment in cities with lower regulations and better infrastructure. Expensive and unreliable power supply reduces the productivity of manufacturing, particularly in the high-tech industries, such as pharmaceutical and electronics, as compared to the resource-based industries. Thus, the concentration of pharmaceutical industry in Maharashtra definitely puts forth a case for state government's support with infrastructure and an even stronger case to continue infrastructural development, along with initiatives in the repeal of the old labour laws. The state can definitely encourage the industry in further research and development, particularly in novel areas such as drug discovery programmes, so that it can reap the highest benefits of the patent regime. Since drug discovery programmes require much larger investment as compared to a generic or contract research and manufacturing business, the state can take initiatives to attract private investment in that area.

6 Conclusion and Policy Recommendations

In order to understand the reform initiatives of the state of Maharashtra in its trade-related policies between 1991 and 2007, the present study starts with a brief outline of the liberalisation initiative of the Centre. Considering the current balance of payment situation, since India does not seem to be as vulnerable to the BOP crisis as earlier, it is expected that the country will continue the liberalisation policy. Panagariya (2008) suggests that the ultimate goal of the country should be to move towards free trade in industrial goods, and to move in that direction, India should reduce the top tariff to not more than 5 per cent by 2010. India needs to address the problems of high tariff in sectors like automobile or some textile items, and in the agricultural sector as well. If India is able to convince the OECD countries to reduce their agricultural subsidies then it can also open its own market through a reduction in tariffs.

Since small firms find it difficult to face the competition and reap the benefits of an open economy due to their isolation and ineffective linkages, a cluster development approach can be adapted. This kind of developmental approach by the governments has been proven to help in some of the developed countries like Germany, Italy and the US. While the Government of India has also started implementing this approach, states like Andhra Pradesh, Madhya Pradesh, Rajasthan, Gujarat, Karnataka, Tamil Nadu and Chhattisgarh, have taken cluster development approach in their industrial policy. Maharashtra needs to consider this aspect if it wants to improve its export competitiveness and reap the fruits of this open economy.

The primary purpose of this study was to explore the initiatives in Maharashtra, along with the state-level institutions responsible for policy-making and implementation. A brief outline of the overall performance of Maharashtra in related areas has been provided as well.

Looking at the growth potential in Maharashtra, it can be recommended that if the state government becomes even a little more proactive in infrastructure development, it will automatically attract investors. Since Maharashtra is home to the country's two busiest ports, development of port infrastructure should have a direct role in expansion of investment and trade volumes. The state can perhaps consider developments of dry ports and increase the number of inland containers in Maharashtra. Harmonisation of classification of goods across borders is also one important factor for the speedy movement of goods. E-governance initiatives can be helpful in this respect. The one like 24-hour online container tracking system in Chennai port—enabling traders to monitor container movements from ports to inland depots—can be implemented. It reduces delays in processing trans-shipments requests. Other than investing in infrastructure, such as ports, highway connectivity, the state government also has a major role in assuring uninterrupted power supply.

On land acquisition, it is recommended that the state frame its own rehabilitation policy like the one laid down by the Orissa government, while acquiring the necessary land from farmers under the guidelines set forth by the Land Acquisition Act, 1894. This can bring a solution to land acquisition issues in the long run. Such is a better way, rather than looking at fast acquisition through private party as a short-term solution, as the latter does not bear the responsibility of rehabilitation as much as the government does. A noticeable fact is that there are about 7,500 applications before the MIDC for land acquisition by the industries in the areas of Nagpur, Kolhapur and Sholapur, substantiating the interest of private investors to expand business in the state.[1]

Other than the infrastructure bottlenecks, the state government should also work for more efficient policy implementation. From 1991 to 2008, only 23 per cent of approved investments were completed along with starting the production (MEDC, 2002a); this ratio needs improvement. Maharashtra being one of the leading states in terms of industrial output, and being the country's commercial hub, the changes in trade-related policy in this state has larger implications on the international trade of

1. *Source:* Seminar on *Export Competitiveness of Maharashtra* held on 12 August 2008 at WTC, as a joint collaboration between WTC and MEDC.

India. The tax anomalies across states can be reduced through state initiatives. A long drawn debate on removal of octroi needs to be resolved fast. Even if the issue is complicated from different dimensions of balancing the collection of revenue with equity and minimum distortion, but as most of the other states in India have already abolished this tax, Maharashtra needs to consider this with utmost importance. The prompt implementation of VAT is another need of the hour, as it will reduce trade distorting tax and prevent movement of existing investment outside the state, such as what happened with Bajaj Auto that was discussed earlier.

Moreover, the state government needs to work on skill enhancement in terms of technical direction and managerial abilities, in order to take advantage of possibilities in the open economy under WTO. As mentioned by the development commissioner of Maharashtra in a recent seminar on export competitiveness of the state,[2] the state government needs to strengthen the Udyog Mitra. The development commissioner also mentioned the need for a Container and Warehousing Policy in the state as part of the Logistics Policy, as well as the setting up of overseas facilitation councils to represent the brand 'Maharashtra state' abroad.

The states of Punjab, Uttar Pradesh and Haryana, have their respective successful state export policies. Maharashtra has started its initiative in this line and has sent a draft of its own export policy to the Ministry of Export Promotion. A recent estimate of MEDC (August 2008) shows that Maharashtra ranks third after Gujarat and Chhattisgarh, with Rs. 3,99,691 crore amount of investment through IEMs, and first in terms of the number of IEMs and employment. The investment through export oriented units (EOUs) in Maharashtra is comparatively low at Rs. 8,149 crore, placing it in second position.

In the 1970s, the closure of several textile mills and the other sick units had created unemployment and setbacks in the Maharashtra economy. Within a few years of economic reform, however, the state has begun to attract investors. In 1998-99, the five states including Maharashtra, Gujarat, Andhra Pradesh, Karnataka and Tamil Nadu, shared more than 50 per cent of total investment in the country. Maharashtra maintained the top position in capital investment and industrial

2. Ibid.

Jenkins, Rob (1999). *Democratic Politics and Economic Reform in India.* Cambridge: Cambridge University Press.

———. (2003). "India's States and the Making of Foreign Economic Policy: the Limits of the Constituent Diplomacy Paradigm," *Publius: The Journal of Federalism* 33(4): 63-82.

Joshi, Vijay and Little, I.M.D. (1996). *India's Economic Reforms 1991-2001.* Oxford Publication.

Kennedy, Loraine (2004). "Contrasting Responses to Economic Liberalization in Andhra Pradesh and Tamil Nadu," in Rob Jenkins (ed.), *Regional Reflections: Comparing Politics Across India's States.* Delhi: Oxford University Press.

Kumar, Sanjiv and Leena Thacker Kumar (1996). "Investing in India: Strategies for Tackling Bureaucratic Hurdles," *Business Horizons*, January-February, 10-16.

Maharashtra Economic Development Council (MEDC) (1999). *Investing in Maharashtra-Trends and Prospects*, Annual Number, September.

———. (2002a). *Monthly Economic Digest*, February.

———. (2002b). *The Economic Reforms of Indian States- A Factual Profile.*

———. (2008). *Economic Escorts to Maharashtra – A Statistical Profile*, August.

Maharashtra Investment Forum (2007). "Maharashtra's Economic Performance and Investment Climate," talking points by Chief Minister of Maharashtra, Mr. Vilasrao Deshmukh, at the CEO Roundtable, June (New York).

Mathew, Anil (2008). "Maharashtra Pharma Aims to be No.1," online publication at *pharmabiz.com*, 13 November.

Mathur, Om Prakash (2005). "Impact of Globalisation on Cities and City-related Policies in India," in H.W. Richardson and C.H.C. Bae. (ed.), *Globalization and Urban Development*. Berlin: Springer. pp.43-58.

Mathur, Vibha (2006). *Foreign Trade in India, 1947-2007: Trents, Policies and Prospects*. New Delhi: New Century Publications.

McMillan, Alistair (2005). "The BJP Coalition: Partnership and Power-sharing in Government," in Katharine Adeney and Lawrence Saez (ed.), *Coalition Politics and Hindu Nationalism*. London: Routledge. pp.13-35.

Mitra, Amit (2007). "Maharashtra, Gujarat Fuels India Inc's Dream," *The Hindu Business Line*, 9 October.

Mukherji, Rahul (2005). "The Indian State Under Globalization: A Research Agenda," background paper for the Ford Foundation's project administrated by the National Foundation of India on *The Indian State and Globalization*.

MVIRDC World Trade Centre (2005). *Export Potential for Auto and Auto Components*. (Mumbai).

Narayanan, Badri G. and Pankaj Vashisht (2008). "Determinants of Competitiveness of the Indian Auto Industry," Indian Council for Research on International Economic Relations, *Working Paper* No. 201, January.

National Council of Applied Economic Research (NCAER) (2003). "Andhra Pradesh: Interstate Commerce and International Trade as Engines of Growth," a background paper for the report, *Sources and Constraints of Economic Growth in Andhra Pradesh*, prepared for the World Bank, January.

Okada, Aya (1998). "Does Globalisation Improve Employment and the Quality of Jobs in India?: A Case from the Automobile Industry," *Research note* No. 3, a research project funded by the Alfred P. Sloan Foundation, MIT, Department of Urban Studies and Planning, October.

Oman, Charles P. (1999). "Policy Competition for Foreign Direct Investment: A Study of Competition among Governments to Attract FDI," *OECD*, April.

Panagariya, Arvind (2008). *India The Emerging Giant.* New York: Oxford University Press.

Pethe, Abhay and Mala Lalvani (2005). "Fiscal Situation in Maharashtra: An Assessment, A Critique, and Some Policy Suggestions", National Institute of Public Finance and Policy, *Working Paper* No. 28, March.

Rao, Govinda M. and Kavita R. Rao (2005): "Trends and Issues in Tax Policy and Reform in India," Tax research unit *Working Paper* No.1, National Institute of Public Finance and Policy.

Rudolph, L.I. and S.H. Rudolph (2001). "The Iconization of Chandrababu: Sharing Sovereignty in India's Federal Market Economy", *Economic and Political Weekly* 36(18): 1541-1552.

Saez, Lawrence (2000). "Economic Liberalization and Federalism: The Case of India," in Nagel, Stuart, (ed.), *Global Economic Policy.* New York: Marcel Dekker Publishers pp.195-217.

———. (2002). "Economic Liberalization and the Transformation of Federal Relations," in *Federalism Without a Centre: The Impact of Political and Economic Reform on India's Federal System.* New Delhi: Sage Publications. pp.135-163.

———. (2005). "Coalition Politics, Religious Nationalism and Public Policy: A Theoretical Examination," in Katharine Adeney and Lawrence Saez (ed.), *Coalition Politics and Hindu Nationalism.* London: Routledge. pp.3-12.

Saquib, Mohammed and Nisha Taneja (2005). "Non-Tariff Barriers and India's Exports in Case of ASEAN and SriLanka," ICRIER *Working Paper* No. 165, July.

Sinha, Aseema (2004a). "The Changing Political Economy of Federalism in India: A Historical Institutionalist Approach," *India Review* 3(1), January.

———. (2004b). "Ideas, Interests and Institutions in Policy Change in India: A Comparison of West Bengal and Gujarat," in Rob Jenkins (ed.), *Regional Reflections: Case Studies of Democracy in Practice.* New Delhi: Oxford University Press.

Sutton, John (2004). "The Auto Components Supply Chain in China and India- A Benchmark Study," LSE STICERD *Research Paper* No. EI34, February.

The Times of India (2009). "Babus to be Protected from Netas," 9 June.

Venkatesan, R. and Sonalika Verma (2000). *Study on Policy Competition Among States in India for Attracting Direct Investment.* New Delhi: NCAER.

Weiner, Myron (1998). "The Regionalization of Indian Politics and Its Implications for Economic Reform," *Journal of Policy Reform* 2(4): 337-67.

World Bank (2006, 2007). *Doing Business Report.*

———. (2004, 2006). "India: Investment Climate and Manufacturing Industry," *Investment Climate Assessment,* November.

World Trade Centre (WTC) (2002, 2007). *WTO Trade Policy Review*.

———. (2008). *Research Study on Export Competitiveness of Maharashtra*, August.

Websites:

http://www.acmainfo.com/outlook/outlooksurvey-5.htm. Accessed on 6 June 2009.

http://www.automonitor.co.in/article/Interview-with-Principal-Secretary,-Industries,-Maharashtra,-VK-Jairath/page1.html. Accessed on 6 June 2009.

http://business.gov.in. Accessed on 6 June 2009.

http://dgft.delhi.nic.in/. Accessed on 6 June 2009.

http://www.doingbusiness.org. Accessed on 6 June 2009.

http://indiabudget.nic.in/. Accessed on 6 June 2009.

http://indiacode.nic.in/coiweb/amend/amend74.htm. Accessed on 6 June 2009.

http://www.maharashtra.gov.in/. Accessed on 6 June 2009.

http://www.maharashtra.gov.in/english/maritime/mtinvestShow.php. Accessed on 6 June 2009.

http://www.midcindia.org. Accessed on 6 June 2009.

http://www.pharmaceutical-drug-manufacturers.com/. Accessed on 6 June 2009.

http://www.smallindustryindia.com/publications/books/clusdev/ch5.pdf. Accessed on 6 June 2009.

Appendices

Appendix A-1

Federal Distribution of Power between State and Centre

State:

Law, order, justice and local governance

Public health and environment

Land and water

Airport, post and telegraph

Some types of taxes

Infrastructure, except national highways

Some aspects related to commerce and industry

Centre:

Administrative functions such as defence, foreign affairs

Labour, quality standards

Railways, shipping, ports

Income tax, customs, excise

Deals with the central bank and public debt

Natural resources

Concurrent:

Inter-state interactions

Labour issues

Education

Environment

Power

Shipping and inland waterways

Appendix A-2

Industrial Zones in Maharashtra in MIDC Areas

Different MIDC areas of the state has been classified in to groups A, B, C, D and D+ according to industrial development as mentioned below.

Group A: Comprising the developed areas, *viz.*, Mumbai Metropolitan Region (MMR) and Pune Metropolitan Region (PMR).
Group B: Comprising the areas where some development has taken place.
Group C: Comprising the areas which are less developed than those at Group B.
Group D: Comprising the lesser-developed areas of the state not covered under Group A/Group B/Group C.
Group D+: Comprising those least developed areas not covered under Group A/ Group B/Group C/Group D.
No-Industry District (NID): As may be specified by government.

Appendix A-3

Incentive Schemes in the MIDC Areas

Table A1

For Exemptions in Electricity Duty

Groups	*Description*
A	100% exemption to IT/ITES/BT/units in SEZ/electronic hardware technology parks, 100% EOU and export processing zone for a period of 10 years.
B	100% exemption to IT/ITES/BT/units in SEZ and electronic hardware technology parks and 100% EOU for a period of 10 years.
C	100% exemption to all new units for a period of 15 years.
D	100% exemption to all new units for a period of 15 years.
D+	100% exemption to all new units for a period of 15 years.
NID	100% exemption to all new units for a period of 15 years.

Source: MIDC website: *http://www.midcindia.org/MIDCWebSite/investment/investscheme.aspx?inav=2*, accessed on 5 June 2009.

Table A2

For Exemptions in Stamp Duty

Groups	*Description*
A	IT/ITES/BT units in public parks. 75 per cent exemption to IT/ITES units in private parks. 50 per cent exemption to BT units in private parks. 90 per cent exemption on the additional instruments of leave and licence agreement executed. 75 per cent exemption to IT/ITES units in private parks. 50 per cent exemption to BT units in private parks. 90 per cent exemption on the additional instruments of leave and licence. Agreement executed by the IT units and ITES units for starting a new information technology unit in IT park in private sector.
B	IT/ITES/BT units in public parks. 75 per cent exemption to IT/ITES units in private parks. 50 per cent exemption to BT units in private parks. 90 per cent exemption on the additional instruments of leave and licence agreement executed. 75 per cent exemption to IT/ITES units in private parks. 50 per cent exemption to BT units in private parks. 90 per cent exemption on the additional instruments of leave and licence. Agreement and transfer of lease executed by any person for starting a new IT unit and ITES unit and a new extension of IT unit and ITES unit.
C	100 per cent exemption to all new units/expansion of units. 90 per cent exemption on the additional instruments of leave and licence agreement executed by the IT units and ITES units for starting a new information technology unit in IT park in private sector.
D	100 per cent exemption to all new units/expansion of units. 90 per cent exemption on the additional instruments of leave and licence agreement and transfer of lease executed by any person for starting a new IT unit and ITES unit and a new extension of IT unit and ITES unit.
D+	100 per cent exemption to all new units/expansion of units. 90 per cent exemption on the additional instruments of leave and licence agreement and transfer of lease executed by any person for starting a new IT unit and ITES unit and a new extension of IT unit and ITES unit.
NID	100 per cent exemption to all new units/expansion of units. 90 per cent exemption on the additional instruments of leave and licence agreement and transfer of lease executed by any person for starting a new IT unit and ITES unit and a new extension of IT unit and ITES unit.

Table A3

Refund of Octroi

Groups	*Description*
A	To all electronic units (including software development) (excluding Mumbai Municipal Corporation, Thane Municipal Corporation, Mira Bhayander Municipal Corporation and Pune Municipal Corporation) for a period of 5 years or the value of the total fixed investment, whichever is lower.
B	To all units for a period of 5 years or the value 100 per cent of the total fixed investment, whichever is lower.
C	To all units for a period of 7 years or the value 100 per cent of the total fixed investment, whichever is lower.
D	To all units for a period of 9 years or the value 100 per cent of the total fixed investment, whichever is lower.
D+	To all units for a period of 12 years or the value 100 per cent of the total fixed investment, whichever is lower.
NID	To all units for a period of 15 years or the value 100 per cent of the total fixed investment, whichever is lower.

Tabel A4

Special Capital Incentives to all SSI Units

Groups	*Description*
A	
B	
C	Ceiling as 20 per cent of fixed capital investment of monetary ceiling Rs. 10 lakh. Disbursement in equal annual instalment over 5 years. Disbursement in one instalment for agro processing units, export oriented units, poultry units, dairy units and units in Gadchiroli and Hingoli districts.
D	Ceiling as 30 per cent of fixed capital investment of monetary ceiling Rs. 20 lakh. Disburse in equal annual instalment over 5 years. Disbursement in one instalment for agro processing units, export oriented units, poultry units, dairy units and units in Gadchiroli and Hingoli districts.
D+	Ceiling as 35 per cent of fixed capital investment of monetary ceiling Rs. 25 lakh. Disburse in equal annual instalment over 5 years. Disbursement in one instalment for agro processing units, export oriented units, poultry units, dairy units and units in Gadchiroli and Hingoli districts.
NID	Ceiling as 40 per cent of fixed capital investment of monetary ceiling Rs.35 lakh. Disburse in equal annual instalment over 5 years.

Table A5

Interest Subsidy to New Textile, Knitwear and Hosiery SSI Industries

Groups	*Description*
A	
B	
C	Monetary ceiling of Rs. 10 lakh for the max. period of 4 years at 5 per cent interest p.a.
D	Monetary ceiling of Rs. 20 lakh for the max. period of 5 years at 5 per cent interest p.a.
D+	Monetary ceiling of Rs. 25 lakh for the max. period of 6 years at 5 per cent interest p.a.
NID	Monetary ceiling of Rs. 35 lakh for the max. period of 7 years at 5 per cent interest p.a.

Index

P

Q

R

S

T

U

V

W